Praise for *No Higher*

"I am not aware of an [...] more extensive and div[...] than John Suthers. Hi[...] [...]norable experience makes this excellent book a must-read for anyone interested in the prosecution function and the complex issues of our criminal justice system."

—Stu VanMeveren, former district attorney, former president
of the National District Attorneys Association

"John Suthers, with his unique credentials as a local, state, and federal prosecutor, offers a balanced critique of the justice system that helps maintain our civil society. *No Higher Calling, No Greater Responsibility* is an easy read about a complex subject. The mix of real-life anecdotes with an intellectual analysis provides an enjoyable yet educational experience for those who are lucky enough to read this outstanding book."

—Stephen Carter, Indiana attorney general and former president
of the National Association of Attorneys General

"...a highly personal account of Suthers' experiences in the justice system throughout his distinguished career. The book offers an insider's perspective on the administration of justice and, most importantly, puts forth original ideas as to how we can become a more just society. I have long admired John Suthers' dedication to the public good, and I recommend this book to anyone who shares that commitment."

—Ken Salazar, U.S. senator and former
Colorado attorney general

No Higher Calling, No Greater Responsibility

A Prosecutor Makes His Case

John W. Suthers

Foreword by Colorado Governor Bill Ritter

FULCRUM

GOLDEN, COLORADO

Library of Congress Cataloging-in-Publication Data

Suthers, John W.

  No higher calling, no greater responsibility : a prosecutor makes his case John W. Suthers ; foreword by Colorado Governor Bill Ritter.

    p. cm. -- (Speaker's corner books)

  ISBN 978-1-55591-662-6 (hardcover)

1. Prosecution--United States. 2. Suthers, John W. 3. Public prosecutors--Colorado--Biography. I. Title. II. Series.

  KF9640.S88 2008

  345.73'05042--dc22

                    2008003465

ISBN 978-1-55591-504-9 (pbk.)

Printed on recycled paper in the United States of America

0 9 8 7 6 5 4 3 2

Design by Jack Lenzo

Fulcrum Publishing

4690 Table Mountain Dr., Ste. 100

Golden, CO 80403

800-992-2908 • 303-277-1623

www.fulcrumbooks.com

Contents

Acknowledgments

I have had the unique privilege of serving as a district attorney, United States attorney, and state attorney general. I tell people I've been lucky enough to win the "legal trifecta." A relatively small number of people have made my career as a local, state, and federal prosecutor possible. But literally hundreds, if not thousands, of people have made that career meaningful and enjoyable.

It was a law student internship in the Fourth Judicial District Attorney's Office in Colorado Springs that convinced me I wanted to be a prosecutor, but it was District Attorney Robert Russel and his assistant district attorney, Ron Rowan, who gave me a job as a deputy district attorney in favor of many other applicants. It was also Bob Russel who promoted me to chief deputy district attorney after less than two years in the office. As a line deputy, many of my colleagues taught me how to be a good prosecutor. Several judges were also encouraging: Matt Railey, Richard Hall, and Bob Johnson, in particular. My staff at the Economic Crime Division showed me how much fun you could have while doing stressful and rewarding work.

When I left the district attorney's office and entered private practice, I had a notion I would run for district attorney at some point. When I did so eight years later, I had broad community support. But it was the strategic work of campaign supporters like Ken Ball, Lianne Shupp, Gil Johnson, Norm Palermo, and my law partner, Ken Sparks, that made my election victory possible. My first official act as district attorney was to choose Jeanne Smith as my top assistant; it was also my best. She did an incredibly good job. She was a great sounding board and was the source of much wisdom during my eight years as district attorney. I was very pleased that she succeeded me as DA and very grateful that she answered my call again when I became Colorado attorney general in 2005. Dozens of outstanding lawyers and support staff manned the Fourth Judicial District Attorney's Office during my two terms, and we accomplished a great deal. I'm grateful to all of them.

You don't become a U.S. attorney without the support of your state's senators, and I'm thankful to Senator Wayne Allard and Senator Ben Nighthorse Campbell for their support. But it was probably Colorado Governor Bill Owens, whose cabinet I had served in for thirty-two months as director of Colorado's Department of Corrections, who was most influential in securing my nomination by President George W. Bush.

The U.S. Attorney's Office for the District of Colorado was a great place to work with many exceptional lawyers and a dedicated support staff. I believe I improved the office considerably by hiring many top-notch attorneys during my tenure. One of my first decisions as U.S. attorney was to appoint Bill Leone, with whom I had briefly practiced law in the mid-1980s, as the first assistant U.S. attorney. Bill is a very intelligent and capable lawyer and served admirably as the interim U.S. attorney after I left the office. Jim Allison, the head of the Criminal Division, was a consummate federal prosecutor and great counsel. Jeff Dorschner, the public information officer, taught me a tremendous amount about effective media relations. My entire management team at the U.S. attorney's office was very competent and dedicated to the task of effectively representing the United States.

It was Governor Owens who asked me to take on the challenge of serving as Colorado attorney general when the office was vacated in January 2005 by Ken Salazar, who had been elected to the United States Senate. Salazar is a Democrat who exhibited considerable statesmanship in supporting my appointment and thereby aiding my confirmation process in the Democrat-controlled state Senate. I have the highly discerning voters of Colorado to thank for my election victory in November 2006, a time when many other Republicans were not faring well. I believe the voters were appreciative of the bipartisan manner in which I have managed the legal work of the state.

My management team at the Colorado Attorney General's Office has done a great job. I'm particularly appreciative of the policy advice I've gotten from Deputy Attorney Generals Jason Dunn, Dennis Ellis, Geoff Blue and Solicitor General Dan Domenico, and for the steady hand of Chief Deputy Attorney General Cynthia Coffman in the day-to-day management of the office. My executive assistants, Judy Evans and Terri Connell, made sure I showed up where I was supposed to and with something marginally intelligent to say, and that's no mean feat. My section heads, Renny Fagan, Diana Black, Beth McCann, Jan Zavislan, Casey Shpall, Jeanne Smith, John Sleeman, and Tom Raynes, have been both admirably loyal and remarkably competent.

I deeply regret that I am able to specifically name just a few of the people who have been instrumental in the success I've enjoyed as a public prosecutor when there are so many people responsible for that success and for making my work as a prosecutor so rewarding. The only means I have of rectifying that omission is in the dedication of this book:

To all the men and women who served with me at the Fourth Judicial District Attorney's Office, at the U.S. Attorney's Office for the District of Colorado, and the Colorado Attorney General's Office and who have so capably and effectively pursued justice on behalf of the people of Colorado and on behalf of the United States of America. They have inspired me and given meaning and purpose to my life much greater than I could ever anticipate and for which I can never adequately express my gratitude.

Foreword

When I became the Denver district attorney in 1993, John Suthers was already highly respected in the ranks of Colorado's DAs. I didn't hesitate to call on him for advice or to exchange ideas. Over the ensuing years, we worked closely together on a wide variety of criminal justice issues, not the least of which was a fundamental change in how Colorado dealt with violent juvenile offenders.

Until I was term limited as Denver's DA in 2005, prosecution was my life's work. It's an incredibly important public responsibility. Effective prosecution is an essential element of good government. Every citizen should have a basic understanding of how our justice system works, and that requires an understanding of the prosecutor's role in that system. This book discusses the fundamentals of crime and punishment and describes, in an easy to understand fashion, how prosecutors can and should work to promote justice. It also thoughtfully examines many critical issues in today's justice system.

John Suthers' legal career has been remarkable. I don't know anyone else who has served as an elected district attorney, presidentially appointed U.S. attorney, and state attorney general. In addition, he's run Colorado's correctional system. This gives John a broad and unique perspective on criminal justice, particularly the relationship between state and federal law.

Even when I've found myself in disagreement with John, I've always found his views to be well reasoned and clearly articulated. This book is yet another example of his ability to explain some complex matters in a way that nonlawyers can fully comprehend. He uses his vast experience as a prosecutor, including particular cases he's been involved in, as a means to illustrate how the system works and how it might be made to work better. That makes for enjoyable as well as educational reading.

While John and I are of different political stripes, as Colorado's governor I value his counsel as attorney general. I enjoy our dialogue about the many important legal issues that face our state. When the occasion calls for it, I won't hesitate to use this book to make my point or to refute those of my friend and colleague.

—Bill Ritter, governor of Colorado

Introduction

Prosecutors in the U.S. justice system exercise immense power. Through the exercise of that power, they can advance justice or perpetrate injustice. A prosecutor can ruin a hard-earned reputation with the careless stroke of a pen or protect one by showing cautious restraint. No one in the United States can be branded a criminal or lose their personal liberty unless a prosecutor determines that to be a just consequence, and serious criminals will not be held accountable if a prosecutor is not sufficiently zealous. Through the exercise of consumer protection powers, a public prosecutor can profoundly impact the marketplace. Because of the power prosecutors wield, and the manner in which they can influence our lives, the prosecution function deserves public scrutiny. Every American should have a basic understanding of the role of prosecutors in our system of justice. I've written this book with that objective in mind. But it's also my goal to discuss the prosecution function in the broader context of criminal justice and make pertinent observations about the workings of our justice system as a whole.

Most of the books I've read by or about prosecutors take a decidedly negative view of the U.S. justice system. Many portray the prosecutor as a white knight or avenging angel leading the fight against a system that coddles criminals and fails to protect the law-abiding public. They read like a campaign brochure for a prosecutor seeking reelection or pursuing higher office, or like some of the speeches I gave when I first ran for district attorney. Antiprosecutor books, on the other hand, tend to portray them as politically ambitious, overzealous, and bent on convictions at the price of justice. They're typically authored by a defense attorney, a defendant, or someone else with an ax to grind. They indict the system by indicting the prosecutor.

If you're looking for a justice-system-bashing book, this probably won't be to your liking. I purposely have waited until the latter stages of my career as a prosecutor to write this book. I wanted my observations and conclusions about various topics to be based, to the extent possible, on thoughtful reflections rather than on the passions that characterize the heat of the battle. That's not to say the book doesn't contain plenty of constructive criticism about the justice system and make numerous suggestions as to how it could be made to work more effectively. I think there is plenty of room for improvement. I'm particularly concerned that the complexities of the system can make a search for the truth a secondary consideration and have adversely impacted the fact-finding capabilities of our juries. Juries are returning too many verdicts that are patently contrary to common sense. I suspect that my views about the federalization of crime and about litigious "activism" on the part of state attorneys general will also be seen as somewhat controversial.

It will be very obvious to the reader that your author is a hard-core prosecutor who opposes legalization of drugs, supports the death penalty, and believes that prisons work. But I'm also an advocate of the constitutional rights of criminal defendants and am critical of those, including criminal justice interest groups, that seem determined to undermine some of those rights. This book's analysis of today's justice system considers the extent to which its inefficiencies are by constitutional design, or the result of public and fiscal policy, or are caused by the failings of its various participants.

My intention is that this be a pro-prosecution book without being an antisystem book. It's about the public prosecution function and its unique role in the justice system. Its essential premise is that our system cannot be effective unless the prosecutor competently evaluates the evidence, makes principled charging decisions, and zealously but fairly pursues prosecution and punishment of serious offenders. I view prosecutors' offices as being at the center of the constant struggle between good and evil that is waged every day by dedicated law enforcement professionals. In this book, I use my prosecution career and my myriad of personal experiences as a catalyst for a wide-ranging discussion about crime and punishment. What motivates criminals? What can we hope to achieve by punishing them? Why so much plea bargaining?

It's also a book that looks into the mind of the prosecutor. What types of people make good prosecutors? What motivates them? What can cause a prosecutor to fall short in carrying out their legal and ethical responsibilities?

I don't pretend to speak for all prosecutors. And I don't pretend to be an expert on every matter and every issue discussed in this book. These are merely my observations and conclusions based on my personal experiences during a thirty-year legal career that has included eighteen years as a local, state, and federal prosecutor. It's my effort to touch upon all the considerations that lead me to conclude that being a public prosecutor is a great honor and privilege—and the best job a lawyer can have.

I. Becoming a Prosecutor

The fact is, good prosecutors are made, not born.

I know for certain when I first thought about becoming a lawyer. I'm less certain about when I began thinking about being a prosecutor. In hindsight, I believe my choice to become a prosecutor was the logical culmination of various influences in my life before I graduated from law school. I have a good friend who claims he became a prosecutor because it was the only job he could find when he passed the bar. He then fell in love with the job and made it a career. Another friend says he consciously chose prosecution because he saw it as a political stepping-stone. A female district attorney I worked closely with told me it was the role in the justice system she felt philosophically most comfortable with. I think that was largely my motivation as well. My story is unique, but I don't think it's unusual. I suspect I'm typical of many lawyers who choose to spend all or part of their career in public prosecution. The fact is, good prosecutors are made, not born.

While my life had a bumpy beginning, I had a warm and loving childhood. I was born to an unmarried woman from Ohio who, when she became pregnant, was sent by her family to Denver to have her baby. That was quite common in 1951. I was adopted when I was one month old by a couple in Colorado Springs. I attended a Catholic grade school for eight years. I was a boy scout and an altar boy who memorized his Baltimore Catechism and went to confession once a month. All my sins were venial, if not trivial.

When I was in the sixth grade, my teacher, Miss Holmberg, selected me to be one of three students in the class to debate a team from the seventh grade. On the appointed day, students from the entire school packed into a small gym to witness the oratorical competition. Several parents attended. The school principal and parish pastor were both in attendance. While I can't recall the precise topic of the debate, it had something to do with the relative merits of public versus private education. Given the audience, my team had the enviable task of arguing the superiority of religious schools. As part of my preparation for the debate, I read several articles, including one in a recent issue of *U.S. News & World Report*, to which my father subscribed. The article discussed the fact that inner-city Catholic schools had higher standardized test scores than urban public schools, despite having considerably larger average class sizes. I didn't cite the article in my principal argument because it didn't address the specific issues that I was to cover in my limited time. However, the opposition made a big deal about large class sizes in religious schools, arguing they adversely impacted the quality of education. So I began my rebuttal argument by pulling out the magazine and quoting relevant research findings that undermined the heart of the opponent's argument. The seventh grade team was rendered somewhat speechless and visibly demoralized. I managed to stay calm and conceal my glee. But beneath the calm exterior, I had a sense of how Perry Mason must have felt when his surprise witness devastated his opposing counsel's case.

After the sixth-grade team was awarded a decisive victory by the judges, the school principal, Sister John Catherine, approached me. She was obviously pleased with my performance. "You did a great job, John," she said. "You really ought to be a lawyer." I didn't know how to respond. No one in my extended family was a lawyer. In fact, I didn't personally know anyone who was a lawyer. That night I asked my parents to clarify exactly what lawyers do.

But I never forgot Sister John Catherine's suggestion. In fact, it was the only career advice I received in my entire life. From that point forward, I paid careful attention to what lawyers did. And I took every opportunity to improve my writing and oratory skills because I understood those were important for lawyers to have.

I also attended a Catholic high school. Despite the fact that my father died very suddenly when I was a freshman, an event that was the most traumatic in my life, I continued to obey all the rules. I was a good athlete and a very good student. I was elected student body president my senior year. But in terms of my eventual career choice, it was one of my teachers, Sister Georgetta, who had the greatest influence on me. I have frequently credited her for inspiring my interest in public service.

Sister Georgetta taught Latin. The best students were required to take two years of Latin and two years of modern language. Sister Georgetta was about eighty years old. She was less than five feet tall. She took her vow of humility so seriously that she never allowed herself to be photographed. But she had total and complete command of the classroom. Her desk in the front of the class was on a foot-high platform so she could see all the students. She had a deck of index cards with the names of all the students in the class, one name on each card. Boys were listed by their last names, girls by their first. She used the Socratic method, constantly asking questions of her students. She would pick a card and call on the student listed. If the student didn't answer correctly within a few seconds, she would draw another index card. Because she would constantly shuffle the deck of index cards, no student could relax, even if they had just been called on. The resulting tension created a classroom dynamic in which even the most mischievous students tended to be attentive and compliant.

As a Latin scholar, Sister Georgetta spent several summers at the Vatican interpreting ancient documents. She was also an expert in Roman history and would intersperse stories about the Roman Empire with her Latin instruction. One day early in my sophomore year, she told a story about how Rome celebrated the return of its conquering armies from foreign campaigns. She described how the citizens of Rome would line the Appian Way and express their adulation as the heroes of the military campaign paraded by. Each hero would stand on his own horse-drawn chariot. But there would be a slave positioned directly behind him whose only job was to repeatedly whisper in his ear, "*sic transit gloria mundi,*" which means "quickly passes the glory of the world." The purpose was to remind the hero that life is short, fame is fleeting, and that the interests of Rome were greater than his self-interest.

For some reason, Sister Georgetta's story impacted me greatly. My father's recent death was my first real confrontation with mortality, and she related the story in such compelling fashion. "Nothing endures but your character," she explained, and took every opportunity to subtly suggest that a life of service to others was more rewarding than material prosperity.

On the night of my high school graduation, I received several honors and awards, including a full academic scholarship to the University of Notre Dame. As I left the auditorium where the ceremony was held, I encountered Sister Georgetta. At the end of a brief conversation, she cautioned me, "Remember John, *sic transit gloria mundi.*"

I never saw Sister Georgetta again. She died a few years later. But I related this story to family and friends on several occasions. In January 1989, on the day I was sworn in as the elected district attorney of the Fourth Judicial District of Colorado, my sister Sharon presented me with a needlepoint she had made that read "sic transit gloria mundi." The needlepoint has hung on the wall near the door of every office I have occupied since that day. It's a constant reminder that character is all that counts and that the difficult decisions I face must be decided on the merits of the issue rather than on what will bring fleeting public approbation. And it provides insight into why it is I have chosen to spend much of my legal career in public service rather than in more lucrative pursuits.

At Notre Dame, I majored in government and international studies. I had several professors who were self-described liberals and a few who were avowed conservatives. Two of the conservatives had the greatest impact on my thinking and my career choices. Professor Paul "Black Bart" Bartholomew taught constitutional law. Unlike so many other teachers I encountered, Bartholomew didn't tout the U.S. Constitution as a means to solve every social problem or societal imbalance. He taught a reverence for the Constitution and the Bill of Rights as a statement of fundamental principles designed to ensure the supremacy of individual freedom vis-à-vis the state. Although his class was generally considered the most difficult in the major, I thrived on it and was the star pupil, according to the letter of recommendation Bartholomew later wrote to law schools. The experience reinforced my desire to become a lawyer.

I took political theory from Professor Gerhart Niemeyer. As I recall the story, Niemeyer had been a member of the Communist Party in Germany. He immigrated to the United States in 1937 with the rise of Hitler and began teaching at Princeton. Over time he became one of the most virulent anticommunists in academia. By the time I took his course at Notre Dame, he was in his late sixties but still a celebrity of sorts, frequently appearing as a guest of William F. Buckley Jr. on his TV show, *Firing Line*.

But it was Niemeyer's conservative view of law and order that intrigued me the most. He discussed the optimistic view of human nature found in the work of Plato and Aristotle, both of whom emphasized man's ability to be virtuous and the role of law to promote the public good. But from my perspective, Niemeyer was fundamentally a Hobbesian. Thomas Hobbes, a seventeenth-century English philosopher and the author of *Leviathan*, believed that humans were instinctively selfish and prone to hedonism. Only a human's instinct for survival is stronger than his evil inclinations. As a consequence, humans choose to live collectively and must create, out of necessity, a "social contract" or set of rules and regulations to control their evil impulses and promote their mutual protection. The alternative is anarchy and chaos. When an individual violates the social contract, the community must impose a punishment that is sufficiently harsh to deter both the offender and other potential offenders within the community. The community chooses one or more among them to enforce the contract. In the modern context, the legislature, as elected representatives of the community, enacts the criminal laws that constitute the social contract. They also determine what sanctions are necessary to deter lawbreaking and promote law and order. Police and prosecutors enforce the social contract. Judges ensure the enforcement is done fairly.

It would subsequently be my experience that most veteran prosecutors were Hobbesian at heart. They tend to have a somewhat pessimistic view of human nature and a belief that vigorous enforcement of the social contract is necessary to prevent the triumph of anarchy and chaos.

With such a mindset, the prosecution function is viewed as being of the utmost societal priority.

It was with this intellectual experience that I entered the University of Colorado Law School in the fall of 1974. Over the next three years, I would be exposed to many areas of the law. But I would read or hear virtually nothing that would encourage me to become a prosecutor. My criminal law–related courses uniformly glamorized the defense function and negatively stereotyped police and prosecutors. Defense attorneys helped free the innocent and protected defendant's constitutional rights from government oppression. Prosecutors were portrayed, in their best light, as a necessary evil prone to overzealousness. My criminal law, criminal procedure, and constitutional law professors had very little practical experience and none had been a prosecutor.

In defense of the University of Colorado Law School, I'm certain my experience was not unusual. I've subsequently found that most law schools, particularly the elite ones, are bastions of liberal thought, and most of the students are content with that. It's only in the past two decades that I've seen some significant push back, primarily through the work of the Federalist Society. Most of my law school classmates had spent the last several years protesting the Vietnam War and enthusiastically embracing the lack of inhibition that characterized the era. I was definitely among the dullest and most politically conservative elements of the law school. So it's not surprising that I learned much more about the practical realities of the law outside of the law school environment.

Each summer during law school, I searched for opportunities to get practical experience. The summer after my first year, I worked as a legal editor for *Shepard's* Citations Service. A neighbor was the editor in chief and helped me secure the job. While I learned a lot of legal terminology and read hundreds of appellate cases, it was uninspiring work. I thought I wanted to be a trial lawyer but had very little notion of how to go about it. My mother had died suddenly during my first year of law school, and, with both of my parents dead, I had very few contacts who could assist me. At Christmas break during my second year, I sought the advice of a state trial court judge who attended my parish church. He strongly recommended I contact the local district attorney's office and seek a summer internship. "There's no better experience," he said. He gave me the name of the top assistant district attorney. That led to an unpaid internship the following summer. I had to work in the landscaping business on Saturdays and Sundays to help make ends meet. During my third year of law school, I was able to continue my internship at the district attorney's office and receive three hours of credit. I was required to meet with an assigned professor once a month to discuss the work I was doing and have him review my written work product.

Throughout my two-year internship at the district attorney's office in Colorado Springs, I spent a great deal of time doing legal research related to a number of notorious murder cases. The first case I worked on was a special prosecution of a murder case in Aspen, Colorado. A transient was accused of kidnapping, sexually assaulting, and murdering a nurse. There was a strong suspicion that the defendant was a serial killer, and the death penalty was being sought. I did a significant amount of legal research on the case until, just days before the trial was to begin, the defendant escaped from jail. He wound up in Florida, where he was eventually tried, convicted, and executed for killing three college coeds. His name was Ted Bundy.

Another case I worked on involved a group of young Army soldiers at Fort Carson who had recently returned from Vietnam. The soldiers had formed a robbery gang of sorts and, incredibly enough, met on designated nights of the week to perpetrate their crimes. Unfortunately, they also made a pact among themselves to kill any victim whom they believed might be able to identify them. Over the course of two months in the summer of 1975, they murdered at least five people. A cook at a local hotel was abducted in the parking lot on his way to his car, taken to a nearby stream, and shot point-blank in the head. The robbery netted $1.50. Another soldier was stabbed to death for a marijuana cigarette. At a party after that killing, the perpetrator, a nineteen-year-old GI named Michael Corbett, displayed the bloody knife, reenacted the killing for those in attendance, and exclaimed how exhilarating it had been to turn the knife in the victim's chest and listen to his bones crack.

But undoubtedly the most heinous murder in the GIs' killing spree was that of Karen Grammer, the younger sister of Kelsey Grammer, who over the ensuing years became a huge television star. Grammer, eighteen years old, was at a Red Lobster in Colorado Springs. The restaurant had closed at 9:00 P.M. and she was waiting for her boyfriend to get off work. The gang of soldiers drove up for the purpose of robbing the restaurant. Finding it closed, they changed their plans and abducted Karen Grammer. They took her to an apartment and took turns raping her. They then drove around discussing, in her presence, what to do with her. Upon concluding they couldn't risk releasing her, a nineteen-year-old GI named Freddie Lee Glenn took her out of the car, stabbed her repeatedly, and slit her throat. They left her for dead in an alley. But she wasn't dead yet. Grammer crawled about fifty yards to a trailer in a nearby trailer park. She attempted unsuccessfully to reach the doorbell, leaving bloody handprints on the side of the trailer. Karen Grammer died in that position, to be found by the trailer's occupant when he awoke the next morning.

After weeks of intense investigation, the police solved the murder cases. The district attorney's office asked for the death penalty for Michael Corbett and Freddie Lee Glenn, believing them to be the ringleaders of the murderous group. Several other defendants pled guilty or were convicted at trial of murder and robbery charges. In highly sensational trials, both Corbett and Glenn were convicted of multiple counts of murder and sentenced to death by juries.

I was commended by the district attorney's office for the work I did researching the many legal issues arising in the murder trials and death-sentencing hearings. I also impressed my supervising law professor. It was clear he had never tried a criminal case and seemed shocked when I showed him crime scene photos, but that didn't keep him from lecturing me in opposition to the death penalty.

My experience as an intern at the district attorney's office had a far-reaching impact on me. I sat through significant parts of the trials of Corbett and Glenn. I had never been exposed to such evil. It was inconceivable to me that anyone could have such casual indifference to human life, and I fully understood the community's outrage at such a heinous breach of the social contract. As a small part of the prosecution team, I experienced the immense satisfaction that prosecutors feel when they are successful in holding a defendant responsible for a reprehensible crime. I recognized that prosecutors in such cases stand as society's only acceptable alternative to vigilantism. They bear the heavy burden of vindicating the interests of both the victims and the public as a whole. I found the work incredibly fascinating and meaningful. And in the course of it, I decided I wanted to begin my legal career as a prosecutor.

II. Criminal Trials

The Prosecutor as Protagonist

Criminal trials are the highest drama in the law, and the prosecutor is an essential player in every such drama.

Nothing seems to capture the attention of the public like high-profile crime stories and the trials at which they reach resolution. I've been an eyewitness to the public's fascination on many occasions during my career.

In a complex criminal investigation, the police attempt to fit together various parts of an evidentiary jigsaw puzzle, hoping to frame a clear picture for the prosecutor, the judge, and the jury. The criminal trial that may result is an adversarial combat of wits played out in a very public forum and in a framework of sometimes intricate evidentiary rules. The media and the public who watch or read the detailed descriptions of the case love the drama and the suspense. Everyone has a role to play, and the prosecutor is the protagonist.

U.S. history is replete with famous criminal trials, many of which help describe the tenor of the times in which they occurred. Ironically, but perhaps not surprisingly, many of the most famous trials in our country's history are famous because a questionable result occurred or a lingering controversy remained after the trial.

Americans' fascination with courtroom drama began a century before the enactment of our Constitution in the Salem witch trials. An eleven-year-old girl, Abigail Williams, lived with her uncle in Salem in the Massachusetts Bay Colony. She began acting very strangely in the winter of 1692, going into convulsions, flailing her arms, and alleging a witch was trying to strangle her. Other children followed her example and told their parents, ministers, and civic leaders that there were witches in Salem who had taken possession of them. Apparently, the children had read a book by Cotton Mather, a well-known Boston minister, about the alleged possession of a family named Goodwin. They all exhibited the same symptoms described in Mather's book.

Incredibly, the controversy led to a series of witch trials that exposed the horrors of mass hysteria in combination with a nonindependent judiciary. Before the hysteria was ended by Sir William Phips, the governor of the colony, after his wife was accused, nineteen men and women had been executed and another fifty-five had pled guilty in order to avoid execution. The founding fathers almost certainly had the horror of the witch hunt in mind when they crafted the Constitution and its Bill of Rights.

The American Revolution produced the first famous court-martial in the soon-to-be nation's history. Major General Benedict Arnold was accused of being too friendly with British loyalists and using military personnel to do personal favors. The court-martial panel cleared Arnold, largely in recognition of his significant contributions to the Revolution, but directed General George Washington to reprimand him. Despite Washington's sensitivity and diplomacy in carrying out the directive, Arnold brooded about this result and the ingratitude he perceived it evidenced, and the seeds of his subsequent treason were sown. For Americans, his name is now synonymous with treasonous betrayal.

Aaron Burr was also a disgruntled patriot. He had served the cause of the American Revolution, rising to the rank of lieutenant colonel, and distinguished himself at the Battle of Monmouth. A lawyer, he was elected to the U.S. Senate from New York. In the presidential election of 1800, he tied with Thomas Jefferson in the electoral vote. After thirty-six ballots, the House of Representatives chose Jefferson, and Burr became vice president. The tie-breaking vote was heavily influenced by a fellow New Yorker, Alexander Hamilton, whose political and philosophical disagreements with Jefferson were surpassed only by his dislike and distrust of Burr. Hamilton further undermined Burr's attempt to become the governor of New York in 1804. The bad blood eventually culminated when Burr killed Hamilton in a gun duel. The spectacle caused his once brilliant career to take a disastrous turn.

A politically ruined man, Burr began to engage in highly suspicious activity. He was eventually arrested and charged with treason by the U.S. attorney. It was alleged he was attempting to assemble a group to invade Mexico, with the ultimate intention of detaching a part of the Southwest from the United States and installing himself as governor. His trial in 1807 was presided over by Supreme Court Chief Justice John Marshall. Burr was acquitted, but the evidence was sufficient to further destroy his reputation in the process. He fled to Europe and spent the next several years pursuing the very scheme he had been acquitted of masterminding.

In 1921, America's favorite pastime, baseball, was racked by scandal. In June of that year, eight Chicago White Sox players stood trial for fixing games. The sensational and circuslike trials ended in the acquittal of all eight, despite the fact the evidence of guilt as to some of them was overwhelming. It was a classic example of jury nullification by sympathetic baseball fans. But criminal justice having failed, swift justice came from another source. A former federal judge, Kenesaw Mountain

Landis, was tasked with the job of cleaning up the game after the "Black Sox Scandal," and he took on the mission with vengeance. He promptly banned all the suspected players from baseball for life, including some who were questionably guilty, like Shoeless Joe Jackson. The notion that many who escape justice in the criminal courts will face justice in other forums, where the burden of proof is lower or nonexistent, is a recurring one.

In July 1925, the Scopes "monkey" trial captured the fascination of the entire nation and proved that lawyers can overshadow litigants on the trial stage. Scopes was a substitute science teacher in Dayton, Tennessee. He was charged with teaching evolution in school in violation of a recently enacted state statute. In reality, Scopes never taught evolution, but he agreed to say he did so that the American Civil Liberties Union (ACLU) could stage a show trial and hire Clarence Darrow, the country's most famous defense lawyer, to defend him. The state also succumbed to showmanship, hiring three-time presidential candidate William Jennings Bryant, a Biblical literalist, to prosecute the case and thereby ensure that the trial would be theatrical and highly entertaining.

One hundred newspaper reporters covered the "monkey trial." WGN Radio in Chicago carried it live. The press coverage was decidedly pro-evolution. The trial culminated when Darrow called Bryant as a witness and the egotistical politician consented to take the stand. Bryant was publicly humiliated in a withering examination by Darrow in which he could not rationally defend a literal interpretation of the Bible. A broken man, Bryant died a week later. Given the drama of the trial and the profile of the lawyers, few people remember that the jury convicted Scopes and fined him $100. The upshot of the trial was that antievolution laws were never seriously enforced, in Tennessee or elsewhere, despite ongoing pressure from creationists.

In 1931 in Scottsboro, Alabama, nine young black men jumped a railcar. Several white teenagers were also on board, and a fight broke out. The whites subsequently told police that the blacks had raped two young white women on board the train. Despite the fact witnesses constantly changed their stories and, in some cases, retracted them, the young black men were convicted at racially charged trials. The defendants became known nationally as the Scottsboro Boys, and the case focused attention on racial segregation in the South. The U.S. Supreme Court eventually reversed the convictions. But in even more sensational and racially charged trials, five of the defendants were again convicted in 1936 and 1937, despite virtually no credible evidence. The prosecution eventually dismissed charges against the other four. Of the five convicted, four were paroled and the fifth, Haywood Patterson, escaped and fled to Michigan, where the governor refused to allow him to be extradited back to Alabama. Many historians view the case of the Scottsboro Boys and the controversy it generated as the genesis of the American civil rights movement.

Arguably the most publicized criminal case of the twentieth century, and certainly the most publicized before the invention of television, was the Lindbergh kidnapping case. On March 1, 1932, aviation hero Charles Lindbergh's twenty-month-old son was kidnapped from the family home in New Jersey. His body was found ten weeks later. In 1934 the police arrested a carpenter, Bruno Hauptmann, and charged him with the kidnapping and murder. He was convicted at trial and executed in 1936. The case was a sad and subsequently oft-repeated example of press sensationalism of a tragedy. The Lindbergh family was so adversely impacted by the pervasive intrusion into their privacy by reporters, photographers, and curious onlookers that they moved to Europe in search of both privacy and safety.

Almost as sensational was the case of accused spies Julius and Ethel Rosenberg. The story, which captured the passions of the early stages of the Cold War, riveted the nation from the time of the Rosenberg's arrest to the date of their execution and beyond. Despite the efforts of many, including their children, to prove their innocence, analysis of Soviet documents made available after the end of the Cold War appear to confirm that Julius Rosenberg was indeed guilty of spying for the Soviets. But the conviction of Ethel Rosenberg rested primarily on the contention that she typed documents for delivery to the Soviets, knowing their treasonous content. That fact was testified to at trial by her brother. But fifty years later, the brother reported in a television interview that he wasn't certain who typed the documents. Throughout the investigation and prosecution, Mrs. Rosenberg resisted every effort to separate her culpability from her husband's. They were both executed on June 19, 1953.

As indicated earlier, some trials become famous primarily because they poignantly reflect the tenor of the times. The political turmoil and civil unrest of the 1960s was exemplified in the trial of the Chicago Seven in the aftermath of riots at the 1968 Democratic National Convention. In response to severe criticism of their handling of protestors at the convention, authorities secured indictments against seven of the leaders of the unrest. The defendants' defiant behavior, as well as that of their antiestablishment defense counsel, William M. Kunstler, produced a circuslike atmosphere at the trial. Unfortunately, the seventy-three-year-old federal trial judge, Julius J. Hoffman, was not up to the task of controlling the spectacle. He charged the defendants with 159 counts of contempt of court. Each of the defendants was convicted by the jury and sentenced to five years in prison, but the convictions were reversed on appeal because of the numerous errors of Judge Hoffman. The defendants were never retried. They were found guilty of contempt of court, but no additional jail time was imposed. The case served as a catalyst for the anti–Vietnam War movement.

Anyone who thought the legal system had matured to the point that grossly oversensationalized trials with questionable results were a thing of the past was proven dead wrong by the O. J. Simpson murder trial in Los Angeles. Simpson, a former football star and national TV sportscaster, was accused of killing his estranged wife and her male companion. The evidence of his guilt, both scientific and circumstantial, was considerable. But the defense turned the trial into a race issue. After almost a year of proceedings, a predominantly African American jury acquitted Simpson on October 3, 1995, after less than four hours of deliberation. Most whites were appalled by the verdict. Most African Americans applauded it. Sixty years after the trials of the Scottsboro Boys, racial issues still profoundly impacted the criminal justice system. And celebrity trials still transfixed the public.

These are just ten of many famous criminal trials in U.S. history, but they're representative of the high drama, sensationalism, and often controversial results such trials can produce. But despite this history, polls indicate most Americans still hold to the opinion that our criminal justice system, with its right to trial by jury, is the best ever devised. They seem to understand and appreciate that the price of a system that emphasizes the rights of the accused and places a very high burden on the government is a certain loss of efficiency. That's not to say that Americans are not highly critical of the system's inefficiencies, as will be discussed in a subsequent consideration of possible criminal justice reforms. And it appears that the public's confidence in our jury system has eroded in the last few decades. But Americans still trust our courts more than most other government institutions. They have a sense that on a day-to-day basis, in courthouses all across the country, the system works about as well as can be expected of an institution that is wholly dependent on human discretion and decision making. In contrast to many other countries, U.S. courts are highly independent and largely corruption-free, and their decisions have a high level of public acceptance.

Virtually every day, in almost every municipal, state, or federal courthouse in the United States, motions are argued and cases are tried to judges or juries with little or no media coverage. While the matter means little to the public at large, it means a great deal to the participants. And as every young lawyer quickly learns, every such adversarial confrontation has the potential to cause an adrenalin rush for the litigants. Every litigation involves at least two parties and often two lawyers who are highly interested in the outcome. As I've learned from considerable experience, litigating over the life or liberty of another human being tends to involve more suspense and more stress on the litigants and their attorneys than a battle over dollars and cents. As a private practitioner, I litigated cases involving millions of dollars. But the suspense created by any such controversy could not, in my opinion, compare to that of a murder case. Criminal trials are the highest drama in the law, and the prosecutor is an essential player in every such drama. In fact, justice cannot be achieved without the work of a competent and ethical public prosecutor. Is it any wonder that so many would-be trial lawyers are drawn to prosecution?

I was sworn in as an attorney in Colorado on October 17, 1977. The following day, my twenty-sixth birthday and my first as a duly appointed deputy district attorney (at the lofty salary of $800 per month), I tried two misdemeanor cases. The first was to a judge. The second was to a jury of six.

In the trial to the court, a man was accused of shoplifting a pair of shoes. He had walked into a department store and gone straight to the shoe department. After waiting for other people to leave the aisle, he took a shoe box off the shelf and examined the contents. He then took off the shoes he was wearing, put on the new shoes, put the old shoes in the shoe box, and returned it to the shelf. He then proceeded to walk directly out of the store without going near the checkout counter. This was all observed by a store security officer and captured on videotape. The security officer stopped the man as he was getting into his car. Upon questioning, he offered no explanation for his conduct. What a great case to start your prosecution career! The female security officer was experienced and did a good job of testifying. The videotape wholly corroborated her testimony. The defendant did not testify. I felt I made a good closing argument and the public defender lacked conviction in arguing for acquittal. But the county court judge who heard the case promptly found the defendant not guilty, indicating he was not convinced beyond a reasonable doubt that the defendant intended to permanently deprive the store of the shoes. I was shocked and somewhat humiliated, at least until my supervisor told me that the judge, the former head of the local public defender's office, routinely acquitted obviously guilty defendants as his way of dealing equity to those he perceived as society's downtrodden. I found that out for myself on repeated occasions during the next several months. I found it somewhat amusing, until the judge acquitted a man of child abuse after he whipped his son with a belt until large welts appeared and started bleeding. At that result, I lost my temper in the courtroom. When I went to see the judge the next day to apologize, he told me not to worry about it and added, "I probably went too far in letting that guy off."

In the afternoon jury trial on my first day as a deputy district attorney, the defendant was accused of growing marijuana in his garden. I was quite nervous about establishing the chain of evidence necessary to get the marijuana plants and the test results admitted into evidence. But the trial went smoothly, and the jury quickly convicted the defendant, despite his protestations that he didn't know the dozen or so large plants in his garden were pot. "We weren't born yesterday," the jury foreman told me after the verdict.

I had learned a valuable lesson on my first day as a prosecutor. For the rest of my career, I would tend to trust the collective wisdom and common sense of juries, although they would sorely test that trust on more than a few occasions, and I would tend to distrust some judges who exhibited a philosophical agenda, particularly in routine cases conducted outside of public scrutiny.

Several months later, in my first two felony trials, I learned another great lesson about being a trial lawyer: sometimes it's better to be lucky than good. My first felony trial was a burglary case, and it was a tough case to prove. The victim's house had been burglarized. The defendant was caught two blocks away with apparent burglary tools, including a screwdriver. An accomplice had been caught at the scene with the victim's jewelry in hand, but he refused to testify against his buddy. The defendant denied he'd been involved in the burglary. It had never occurred to me to have the victim look at the burglary tools recovered from the defendant. But when she took the stand to testify, the screwdriver, already admitted into evidence, was on the table next to the witness stand. When she sat down and happened to glance at the table, she exclaimed, "Hey, that's my screwdriver," and proceeded to point out distinctive markings on it. Case closed.

In my second felony trial, the defendant was charged

with robbing a convenience store. Although picked out of a photo lineup by the store clerk, he claimed he'd never been in the store in his life. The store clerk was on the stand and testified that there were two customers in the store when the suspect entered. At that, the defendant leaned over to his defense counsel and whispered, loud enough for several jurors to hear, "There were three." The defense attorney sunk in his chair. Again, case closed. Trial lawyers must learn to expect the unexpected.

Over the ensuing decades, I would personally try a few hundred cases to the court and approximately sixty cases to a jury, including six first-degree murder cases. As district attorney, U.S. attorney, and attorney general, I would be emotionally involved in hundreds of other trials my office prosecuted. I vividly recall the facts of every high-profile case in which I was personally involved, and, with a little prompting, I can relate the essential facts of almost all the major cases my office took to trial. Such recollections are common among trial lawyers. Working as a trial lawyer is both a stressful and memorable undertaking.

Much of the stress of being a trial lawyer arises from the inherent unpredictability of the process. That can be particularly tough on young prosecutors because they have not yet come to fully understand and appreciate the jury's narrowly defined task in a criminal case and precisely what a not-guilty verdict means. I frequently read newspaper headlines or hear TV reporters proclaim that a jury has found a defendant innocent. It drives me crazy. In fact, of course, juries don't decide whether a defendant is guilty or innocent. Webster defines innocence as "not having done .what one is accused of doing." That's not what juries determine. In the U.S. system, a defendant is presumed innocent unless and until proven guilty beyond a reasonable doubt. The only question for a jury in a particular criminal case is whether the prosecution has met its very high burden and convinced all the members of that particular jury that the defendant committed the crime he's charged with. If they don't, the jury acquits the defendant by finding him not guilty. While that allows him to retain the presumption of innocence, the jury never makes an affirmative finding that the defendant did not in fact commit the crime. They don't find the defendant innocent. In my entire career, I've never had a juror tell me, after a not-guilty verdict, that they were convinced the defendant "didn't do it." I'm sure it happens, but jurors have always told me they weren't convinced beyond a reasonable doubt, or they frequently cite some higher nonlegal standard, such as "beyond a shadow of a doubt."

When I have taught at beginning prosecutor courses or at law enforcement academies throughout my career, I have always emphasized to the class that if they want to retain their sanity, they must understand what a not-guilty verdict means and what it doesn't mean. And they have to understand that when a defendant pleads not guilty, very rarely is he saying, "I didn't do it." Almost always he's saying, "Prove it." That's his constitutional right. And it's their job to gather the evidence and, if necessary, present the evidence in court in order to prove it. And it's the process of trying to prove that a defendant is guilty as charged that makes the job of a prosecutor as challenging and exciting an undertaking as the law affords.

III. The Criminal Law
The Ten Commandments versus the Seven Deadly Sins

Virtually all the misbehavior the criminal law proscribes can be attributed to a few basic vices that have always plagued the human race.

When I was a young boy contemplating whether to do something I knew I wasn't supposed to do, the law was the least of my concerns. If my contemplated misdeed involved moral turpitude, like telling a lie, I feared God's consequences as well as my parents'. In fact, one of my earliest recollections involves an incident at a grocery store when I was four or five years old. While shopping with my mother, I asked her to buy a candy bar for me. When she refused, I clandestinely took the candy bar off the shelf and put it in my pocket. When I got home I took it out of my pocket to eat. But I was so overcome with guilt and fear of the fires of hell that I promptly confessed to my mother. She immediately drove me all the way back to the store and took me to the manager. I paid for the candy bar out of my allowance of ten cents per week. As a result of that experience, I can honestly say I was never seriously tempted to steal anything again.

Throughout my legal career, I have given numerous speeches lamenting the declining role of the family, the school, and the church in defining and upholding public morality. I have talked about the need to cultivate virtuous citizens and the need to restore obedience to the unenforceable. And I have railed against prime-time television and other assaults on our national culture. But it was an interview with a job applicant that caused me to focus more clearly on the impact of our declining moral ethos. When I asked a young attorney applicant why she was attracted to prosecution, she replied quickly and forthrightly, "From my perspective, Mr. Suthers, the criminal law is about the only moral code left in our society. I think it's important we rigorously enforce it." Upon reflection, I found her answer sobering. I was reminded of a response I had recently given to someone who asked me the difference between being a district attorney and being a U.S. attorney. One of the differences, I explained, was that the district attorney enforces the Ten Commandments, or at least the three or four commandments presently incorporated into the criminal law. The U.S. attorney, on the other hand, typically enforces the fine print, which includes a myriad of federal rules and regulations not always commonly understood by the average person.

Sadly enough, it does appear that way too many Americans have no other code of conduct than the criminal law and no source of deterrence to bad conduct other than punishments the law affords. In such a circumstance, police and prosecutors have become, by default, the enforcers of the only moral code with a high level of societal consensus. Under such an ethic, if it's not illegal, it's acceptable.

I've often heard people say, "You can't legislate morality." But that's exactly what the criminal law does. The issue is whether there is sufficient consensus among the people that behavior is immoral and should be illegal. Because there remains overwhelming consensus that murder, rape, and robbery are immoral, they remain illegal. It's only when a consensus about the morality of behavior is lost that such behavior is likely to be decriminalized.

Human civilization has changed a lot in the last five thousand years, but my prosecution career has convinced me that human nature has not. Virtually all the misbehavior the criminal law proscribes can be attributed to a few basic vices that have always plagued the human race. The misbehavior may change, but the motive does not.

I was a founding member of the St. Thomas More Society, a Catholic lawyers' guild, in Colorado Springs. The group met periodically to discuss issues of import to our lives as lawyers and Christians. We had a series of discussions about the subject of character, asking the profound question of whether a good lawyer can be a good Christian. We also had a series of seven sessions devoted to a consideration of the seven deadly sins. In the course of lively discussions on greed, pride, lust, anger, envy, gluttony, and sloth, I came to a realization that I'm sure was apparent to whoever identified them as the cardinal sins in the first place. Each of the sins entails a fundamental weakness or deviance of human nature, and collectively they describe the motive for virtually all the behavior society chooses to make criminal. With some thought, it was apparent to me that just about every serious criminal case I've been involved with entailed one or more of the seven cardinal sins.

Greed

Greed is the vice that is most easily and readily identified as the explanation for a wide variety of criminal acts. Most white-collar crimes and a significant portion of property and even violent crimes are ultimately motivated by greed.

As U.S. attorney, my office prosecuted one of the large corporate fraud cases that scandalized the country and undermined the stability of its financial markets in 2001 and 2002. Executives at Qwest Communications were accused of accounting frauds that overstated the company's revenues by more than $2.5 billion. Shareholders and Qwest pensioners lost hundreds of millions of dollars. The motive—pure greed. Qwest executives made millions of dollars on stock options. The CEO made more than $200 million in two years. To do so, they made aggressive quarterly revenue projections that influenced Wall Street analysts, and their underlings had to engage in various accounting chicanery to meet those projections and keep the stock price at artificially inflated levels.

As district attorney, U.S. attorney and attorney general, my office prosecuted numerous investment scams in which greed-driven defendants found very creative and ingenious ways to seduce greed-driven victims to part with their money. Some of the schemes promised investment returns that only a person blinded by greed could have deemed possible.

But greed is not a vice exclusive to the rich. Many a burglary, robbery, or embezzlement perpetrated by persons of limited means are motivated not by necessity, but by covetousness of material possessions. I prosecuted a person on welfare for first-degree murder. She took in an elderly transient woman in order to steal her social security checks. When she found the woman a nuisance, she beat her and eventually buried her alive. In another case, I prosecuted a bookkeeper making $40,000 per year in salary who embezzled $300,000 in six months. She bought a new house, a new car, and a new boat before an auditor discovered her misdeeds.

Greed will always be with us, and so will the crimes it engenders.

Pride

Pride is also a sin behind much criminal behavior. Again, both rich and poor engage in illicit conduct to compensate for feelings of inadequacy or to seek a status different from that which can be legally attained. I have prosecuted thieves who stole not for the money, but to prove their capability. Some corporate officers who commit fraud seem motivated by the status of being among the most highly compensated and seemingly successful executives. I have prosecuted violent criminals whose sole motive was to prove just how tough they were. In one case, two teenage boys confronted an elderly man in the parking lot of a drugstore and robbed and killed him to prove their worthiness to join a gang. In another case, a young man killed a rival in a drive-by shooting because the victim "dissed" his brother. Pride appears to be the sin behind much gang-related criminal behavior.

But it's also my opinion, albeit a controversial one, that pride is the motivation behind some criminal activities in which one would not expect to find it. Through the years, I prosecuted several cases of civil disobedience, typically by pacifists at military bases or nuclear facilities. At first blush, the defendants appear to be anything but prideful people. But close examination of some of the cases, in contrast to historical incidents of civil disobedience, indicate otherwise, at least to me. In one case that turned out to be much more high-profile than I ever could have imagined, three Dominican nuns were charged by my U.S. attorney's office with cutting through a fence at a nuclear facility, hammering a missile silo, and pouring vials of blood on it. The nuns were dressed in hazmat suits, and United States Air Force security had no idea what they were dealing with until they apprehended the women and determined their identity. On its face, it appeared to be an act of protest against U.S. nuclear policy by three people very committed to their cause. And, indeed, it was. The judge, the jury, and the prosecutor, for that matter, were convinced of that. But it also became clear that it was a publicity stunt. The nuns had essentially taken on such protests as their ministry and clearly reveled in the notoriety it brought them. They each had numerous arrests and convictions for trespass and destruction of property. They had previously always been prosecuted by state and local authorities and never done more than a few months in jail for any offense. The Air Force and the Federal Bureau of Investigation (FBI) asked us, in light of their past records, to charge them with federal crimes for destruction of government property and interference with defense operations, both felonies. We did so. The nuns and their handlers seized the opportunity to transform the case into a national news story. They refused to bond out of jail prior to trial, but regularly sought out media interviews. Pacifist websites rallied the faithful to letter writing campaigns. They retained a very high-profile, very vocal, and very antiestablishment Denver defense attorney to lead their defense team. He contributed greatly to the celebrity of the matter. The defense sought, unsuccessfully, to use international law and a Nuremberg defense at trial. Of course, they couldn't consider plea offers that would have given them a year in jail, because a trial was the stage they were seeking.

At the trial, the nuns made well-scripted, legally irrelevant, tearful, and defiant pleas to the jury. Sensing that the spectacle was about more than peace-loving nuns, the jury was largely unsympathetic and convicted each of them of two felonies. The nuns then had a problem. Because of their past records, the federal sentencing guidelines called for substantial prison terms. Rather than accepting their fate as the natural by-product of their civil disobedience, they once again put their PR machine in high gear. They reluctantly bonded out of jail pending the sentencing to ostensibly bid farewell to loved ones. Instead, they embarked on a whirlwind tour of the country, holding press conferences and media interviews. Letters from supporters poured into the judge and onto editorial pages. Undaunted, the judge sentenced the nuns to prison terms ranging from two and a half to three and a half years. Their fifteen minutes of fame was over, at least for a few years. Their supporters, while claiming they were every bit as committed to the cause as the nuns, seemed very content to hold subsequent protests outside the fence and exercise their First Amendment rights in a lawful and peaceful manner.

The nuns' supporters would surely characterize them as humble and unpretentious. They certainly would not consider them prideful. But having read about the civil disobedience of many others, from Gandhi to Martin Luther King Jr., I'm skeptical. I believe they enjoyed the limelight too much. Crimes motivated by pride can take many forms.

Lust

Many experts contend that lust is rarely the primary motive for sexual assaults. I agree with that contention. Rapists seem motivated more by a need for power and control than by lust. Sexual assaults on children are often the product of compulsive deviance. But make no mistake about it, lust is behind a great deal of criminality. The sin of lust is a passionate desire that is wholly egocentric. While lust is not always sexual in nature, I would rank sex as second only to money in contributing to serious misbehavior, including murder. Men seem predominantly, but not exclusively, vulnerable. One of the most high-profile homicide cases in my prosecution career made the point.

Brian Hood was an insurance agent in Colorado Springs. A former all-American football player, he was tall and good-looking. He claimed to be a born-again Christian, and that was a big part of his persona and his insurance business customer base. His wife, Diane, was a former college cheerleader. They had two children.

Jennifer Reali was a bright and attractive woman who had graduated from college with honors. She was married to an Army captain stationed at Fort Carson in Colorado Springs, and they also had two young children.

Both Brian Hood and Jennifer Reali were unhappy in their marriages. Reali was somewhat depressed about leading the life of an Army wife. Hood, on the other hand, had a dark side. He'd been cheating on Diane ever since she'd gotten pregnant by him before they were married.

Brian Hood met Jennifer Reali in a hot tub at a local fitness center. He convinced her to let him come by her house and provide some information about insurance policies. They wound up having sex on top of a washing machine. (The prosecutors in my office nicknamed Hood the "Maytag Man.") The ensuing torrid affair led to Hood convincing Reali to kill his wife. She dressed up in Army fatigues with a ski mask over her face and confronted Diane Hood as she was leaving a meeting at a local community center. Reali feigned that the motive was to steal Diane's purse before shooting her at almost point-blank range as she begged for her life. Reali then fled the scene, ditched her disguise, picked up her kids from day care, and went home to cook dinner for her family. The next morning, a tearful Brian Hood told the media he hoped law enforcement would find the "evil scum" who killed his wife. Unfortunately for him, they did.

Jennifer Reali worked part-time at a florist shop. The owner of the shop, after reading about the murder, called the police to report that a guy named Brian Hood frequently called Reali at work and stopped by the shop on occasion to see her. One time, he saw them kissing in the alley behind the shop. At about the same time, ballistic test results came back on the bullet that killed Diane Hood. It was shot from an antique gun. The police discovered that Reali's husband had an antique gun collection.

When they interviewed him, he informed them that Reali had asked him, on the day after the murder, to put one of the guns in a safe-deposit box. He retrieved it for them and it was determined to be the murder weapon. The police confronted Reali and, after several hours of questioning, she eventually confessed and provided elaborate details as to how Hood had convinced her to kill his wife. He had read her Bible passages to persuade her that adultery and murder were sins of equal magnitude and that God would forgive them of both. Curiously, he also convinced her that divorce was not an option for him because he was a born-again Christian and it would be "bad for business."

When Brian Hood was arrested, his high-priced lawyer very publicly asserted a "fatal attraction" defense. He admitted the affair but alleged he had tried to break it off and Reali had killed his wife in revenge. The separate trials of Hood and Reali were among the most sensational and scintillating in the history of Colorado. They became the subject of a book, *Sweet Evil*, by Stephen Singular. Reali was convicted of first-degree murder. Hood was convicted of conspiracy to commit first-degree murder and solicitation of first-degree murder. They both have plenty of time in prison to contemplate the consequences of their lustful impulses.

The Internet has brought a new dimension to the cardinal sin of lust. While it has brought about the capability for average Americans to quickly access an incredible amount of information about almost anything, it didn't take long for sinister elements of society to also recognize the Internet's capabilities. Sex-obsessed Internet users have polluted cyberspace. Pornography is rampant. Sexual predators use the Net to cultivate and pursue potential victims. Other users suffer the barrage of sexually explicit solicitations. During my tenure as U.S.

attorney, we routinely prosecuted perverts who contacted children on the Internet and traveled across state lines or international borders to pursue them. We also prosecuted those who used it to distribute obscenity on a mass basis. In one case, the arrest of an Internet-savvy pedophile led to the arrest of an entire Internet-based organization of sixty pedophiles in eleven countries that systematically recruited child victims and exchanged information about them among the predators.

As attorney general, I initiated a "Safe Surfing" initiative designed to educate children and their parents about the dangers posed by criminals on the Internet and to propose changes in the law to assist law enforcement in deterring them. For the foreseeable future, the job of protecting the public from Internet predators will be a difficult and demanding one.

Anger

Anger is another cardinal sin that often leads to disastrous consequences. Uncontrolled rage appears much more common among men than women and is one of the vices behind the domestic violence that plagues our society. I vividly recall a domestic violence incident when I was district attorney that I have often referred to as a prosecutor's worst nightmare. A woman made an appointment to see me. She was being harassed by a very angry ex-husband, a former Colorado Springs police officer. And she was doing everything right. She had procured a restraining order against him. He had violated the restraining order by putting a hose through a window and flooding her basement, and he had been arrested and jailed. She came to tell me that she knew him well enough to know that his anger was out of control. She told me that if he was able to make bond, she was confident that "someone would die." I alerted the deputy handling the case, and she was able to secure a $10,000 bond, approximately four times higher than normal for a misdemeanor of that nature. The judge refused to raise the bond any higher despite the ex-wife's concerns. The defendant posted the bond, and two days later he broke into his ex-wife's house. He raped her at gunpoint in front of their children and then put the gun to his head and killed himself. When I learned that her prediction had come true, I actually thanked God he was dead rather than the woman and her children. I've seen many other cases where an angry abuser killed his whole family before killing himself. And, unfortunately, as we now know, violence begets violence, and the children who grow up in the midst of such anger are more likely to perpetrate violence themselves.

Two other cases I personally handled dramatize the damage that can flow from unchecked anger. Malcolm Perkins, a man in his midthirties, had been plagued by an uncontrolled temper all his life. On the day in question, he was driving up an access ramp onto an interstate highway. His wife and daughter were in the car. An unsuspecting copier repairman inadvertently cut him off. An enraged Perkins caught up with him on the highway, screamed obscenities, and, according to an eyewitness trailing behind them, held up a gun. The repairman then suddenly exited to the left and, as he did so, gave Perkins the finger. A further enraged Perkins veered off the interstate and drove across a field to get on the same road as the repairman. When he caught up with him about a mile and a half later, he pumped six bullets into the repair truck, killing the driver.

At trial, Perkins claimed self-defense. But that was undermined by several witnesses, including another driver that testified Perkins had once chased him down on the same stretch of highway and beat him up after he had cut Perkins off in traffic. Perkins was sentenced to forty-eight years in prison. A number of years later, when I was executive director of the Colorado Department of Corrections, I visited an anger management class at one of the prison facilities. Appropriately enough, Perkins was in the class.

In the first high-profile jury trial I ever tried, Ricky Mateos, a well-educated but underachieving young man, engineered the kidnapping and robbery of a wealthy restaurant owner. The motive? He had been fired from a waiter's job at the restaurant and desperately wanted revenge. He had previously arranged the armed robbery of another restaurant that fired him. While revenge involves premeditation, anger is often at the root of it.

Anger is also behind what are commonly referred to as hate crimes—crimes committed against people because of their race, creed, or ethnicity, or crimes against the government or an agency thereof in retaliation for a perceived wrongdoing. As U.S. attorney, my office convicted four people of burning down a building housing an Internal Revenue Service office to manifest their opposition to U.S. tax policy. Timothy McVeigh's bombing of the federal building in Oklahoma City is another dramatic and deadly example. Having dealt with a number of hate crimes throughout my career, I have developed a fairly reliable profile of the perpetrators. They are typically male, occupational underachievers who see themselves as victims. In their mind, racial, ethnic, or religious minorities have deprived them of opportunities, or the government has erected barriers to the success they deserve. Hate crime has found an ally on the Internet, which provides an inexpensive means for malcontents to search out and readily communicate with like-minded people. The reinforcement helps strengthen and perpetuate the lunacy.

Envy

I'm aware of both violent and property crimes that can be attributed to the cardinal sin of envy. While sometimes difficult to distinguish from anger, jealousy, and other similar human emotions, the covetousness that people feel at the loss of a relationship or due to the desire to possess some tangible thing can grow to unhealthy proportions. In several cases I've prosecuted, the only explanation offered by an ex-husband or boyfriend for killing or seriously injuring an ex-spouse or girlfriend has been, "If I can't have her, nobody can." Later in this book, I relate the story of an Air Force officer who was inattentive to a long-term girlfriend until she went out with another guy. He wound up murdering the rival. I also recall a case in which a man shot a fellow employee due to the envy he experienced when the fellow employee got a promotion he wanted. Envy was probably behind the assassination of a Georgia sheriff by an unsuccessful candidate in the previous election. And what about figure skater Tonya Harding convincing a boyfriend to physically attack a rival in order to enhance her chances in a championship competition?

Other examples of envy are less dramatic but still puzzling. I prosecuted a wealthy woman for stealing a one-of-a-kind piece of jewelry from another woman. In other cases, an accountant who was a stamp collector stole some valuable stamps from a client's collection, and an envious middle-aged man stole a valuable baseball card collection from his neighbor. In several closing arguments I've given or witnessed, the motive was called jealousy, but envy was the cardinal sin involved.

Gluttony and Sloth

It might seem difficult at first to identify criminal behavior rooted in the cardinal sins of gluttony and sloth. They're readily recognizable vices, but rarely associated with crime. Gluttony is self-indulgence usually stemming from an attempt to satisfy an unfulfilled need, even if temporarily. Gluttony often leads to addictions. Sloth is apathy and indifference that leads one to disengage from routine expectations of life. Given these descriptions, I would tend to identify crimes involving substance abuse and crimes committed by substance abusers as related to either or both of these deadly sins. While drug dealers are typically motivated by greed, many illicit drug users are seeking an escape and searching for an alternative reality to their life. The same is true of alcoholics.

Substance abuse exacts a tremendous toll on our society. Crime is only one of many social problems attributable to it. It is both a serious public health issue and a criminal justice issue. Calling substance abuse a sin may not be the way many treatment counselors would approach the problem, but I'm comfortable in asserting that there is a moral dimension to these basic human failures that are seriously undermining public health and safety. I'm distressed that so many "good" parents continue to make little or no effort to teach their children about the dangers of substance abuse. More often than not, I find that they suffer from a gluttonous addiction themselves. It seems every time I think we're starting to make progress in the battle against substance abuse, another horror story tends to disabuse me of that notion. But, as a subsequent segment on drug legalization indicates, I'm unwilling to give up the fight.

Yes, the seven cardinal sins explain virtually all the evil perpetrated by mankind. And the bottom line is that police and prosecutors, as the enforcers of the social contract, are engaged on a daily basis in a battle between good and evil, between virtue and vice. Murder is evil. Rape is evil. Theft is evil. Spending your days fighting evil can be very satisfying work, even for lawyers. Prosecutors are among the small segment of our society that can honestly say that fighting evil is a major part of their job description. That explains why so many surveys of the legal profession indicate that prosecutors have the highest job satisfaction ratings. The discretion that prosecutors exercise daily is unlike that of any other lawyers. They have the responsibility of deciding when to bring a case and, when the lack of evidence or other infirmity in the case makes it appropriate, when to dismiss a case. They also typically have broad discretion, through a plea bargain, to fashion a disposition of a case that ensures the punishment fits the crime. "You're driving the bulldozer," my supervisor once told me when I was a young deputy district attorney. "You can stop it at any time. You can use it to push or shape a proper result, or you can try to bury your opposition, as justice requires," he said. Over time I've come to appreciate his analogy. No other litigator, beholden to the interests of an individual client and not to the public interest, can exercise that kind of discretion. Only a prosecutor can describe his job in that fashion.

IV. Punishment
"A Pound of Flesh" versus "The Quality of Mercy"

The vast majority of Americans never commit a serious criminal offense precisely because they fear the consequences, both legal and nonlegal.

Arguments about the purpose of punishment are as old as civilization. Some of the arguments are reflected in literature in an eloquent way, such as the opposing viewpoints of Shylock and Portia in Shakespeare's *The Merchant of Venice*. Shylock, the moneylender, sought a "pound of flesh" from the merchant Antonio for his failure to repay a debt, asserting that revenge was proper for the injustices he, as a Jew, had suffered at the hands of Antonio and his ilk. Portia, the female lawyer disguised as a man, waxed eloquently to the duke sitting in judgment about "the quality of mercy" and the social benefits derived from it. Historically speaking, both viewpoints have carried the day in different times and different places.

Most of what I've read and heard about the proper role of punishment in criminal justice came from a sociology textbook in college, from law review articles and legal treatises I read in law school, and from being present at hundreds of sentencing hearings and listening to lawyers, judges, defendants, and victims express their views about what should happen in a particular case. In preparing sentencing arguments, I would frequently reflect about the purpose of punishment. But the issue of appropriate punishment became a much more compelling one for me when I was appointed executive director of the Colorado Department of Corrections in January 1999 and spent the next three years in charge of the state's prisons, parole system, and community corrections program. In such a job, when $500 million of taxpayer funds are being allocated to incarcerate thousands of criminals, reality confronts theory.

On the basis of my experience as a prosecutor and corrections administrator, I recognize five possible objectives to be achieved in punishing someone who has violated the criminal law: retribution, restitution, rehabilitation, deterrence, and isolation. I have also formed opinions about how effectively these objectives can be accomplished in today's justice system.

Retribution

It is my view that retribution is a fundamental and appropriate purpose of punishment in the criminal law. While that seems axiomatic to me, not everyone agrees. This position puts me at odds with my own religion, Catholicism, at least as the church's view has been articulated in recent statements by various bishops' conferences. The church says we should never seek retribution or vengeance for crimes committed against us. While I understand that contention on a personal level, on a societal level I believe such a position is intellectually misinformed from a sociological and psychological standpoint. Based on my own intellectual inquiry and, most importantly, my real life experience, I view retribution as playing a very important role in criminal sentencing. Ask yourself, why do we have a criminal justice system in the first place? Whether you share Plato's optimistic view of human nature or have a more cynical Hobbesian view of the world, you'll likely conclude that we have such a system to bring order to the process by which persons aggrieved by behavior that is unacceptable to the community can get redress without taking direct action themselves against the offender. As part of the social contract, we agree to forego vigilantism, or personal vengeance, which would foster anarchy and chaos, and to let the police and prosecutor act for us and the community as a whole in seeking retribution for the misdeed that has caused injury to us. We agree to allow due process to take its course. In this way, societal retribution is at the essence of criminal punishment.

It has also been my observation that retribution can be accomplished in different ways in different types of cases. Retribution for heinous violent crimes usually entails a long period of incarceration. The viability of the social contract demands it. But for a corporate executive charged with securities fraud, the victims and the public as a whole may be more likely to view the prosecution itself and the humiliation of the fall from grace that it entails as meeting their need for retribution and to then be more interested in restitution as a proper punishment. It may well depend on how personally the loss is felt by the victims. It was my experience as an economic crimes prosecutor that white-collar criminals are more apt to "wear the evidence," meaning that the stress of the ordeal is apparent in their appearance and their demeanor and in the conduct of their life after their misbehavior.

Sometimes, as in the case with minimum mandatory sentencing, the law itself will dictate the extent to which retribution is a factor in sentencing. Oftentimes, the judge will make that decision.

Restitution

Restitution is another goal of punishment about which, in my opinion, there is considerable misunderstanding. The theory and the reality of the concept don't always mesh. Everyone views restitution as laudatory and a fundamental concept in punishment, but some see it as a cure-all.

Restorative justice has been hailed by many would-be criminal justice reformers as the answer to the problem of overcrowded jails and prisons. Let the criminal make his victim "whole," financially and otherwise, and both will be restored by the experience, says Charles W. Colson's Prison Fellowship and other similar groups. Restitution certainly has its place, but, in my view, such reformers grossly overstate the value of restorative justice as a means of conflict resolution in certain kinds of cases. Restitution should play a very important role in sentencing in many cases and virtually none in others.

Suggest to a victim who's been robbed of $10 at gunpoint that the perpetrator pay them back the $10 in lieu of incarceration, and they will likely and rightfully be angry. Suggest to a rape victim that the rapist pay for counseling as a means of making her whole, and she will likely and properly be outraged. Only retribution and isolation of the defendants are likely to give solace to these victims.

On the other hand, I clearly recall a controversial sentencing hearing I was involved in as a chief deputy district attorney in charge of the Economic Crime Division. A smooth-talking disbarred lawyer from North Dakota had come to Colorado Springs selling limited partnership interests in a gasohol plant he was allegedly building. He raised $750,000 in less than a month. The investors were all college graduates, including many with advanced degrees. They included the superintendent and commandant of the United States Air Force Academy. As it turned out, a production facility of that nature was not technologically and economically viable at the time, and the crook had violated almost every state and federal securities law on the books. He had squandered all the money on a lavish lifestyle. I had charged him with several felonies, and he'd pled guilty and was set to be sentenced. The probation department had done a thorough background investigation that revealed the defendant to be a classic con artist. He was quite intelligent but hadn't done a legitimate day's work in fifteen years. He lived from one scam to another. I asked for a five- to ten-year prison sentence. The victims, even after reading the presentence report, were outraged. Their economic self-interest trumped any desire for retribution. They wanted him out making money to pay them back, even if that meant he might well rip off someone else. They made passionate appeals to the judge to put him on probation, and accused me of trying to revictimize them. The judge agreed with my assessment that the defendant was unlikely to earn sufficient restitution through any legitimate means. He sentenced him to six years in prison and ordered him to make restitution as a condition of parole. I hope the victims didn't stand by their mailboxes waiting for the checks to come.

If a crime involves an economic loss, whether it be a violent or white-collar crime, then a restitution order should be part of the sentence. And it's now mandated to be under state and federal law, even if the defendant goes to prison. In one federal case I handled on appeal, the trial judge refused to order restitution of $14 million against a forest service worker, Terry Barton, who had started a fire that burned 150,000 acres, including several dwellings. She had a lengthy prison sentence, and the judge, noting she would have limited ability to pay even upon her release, refused to "condemn her to a life of poverty." The Tenth Circuit Court of Appeals told him he was legally obligated to order the restitution. That's a good development in the law. But I think most prosecutors will tell you that restitution has its limits as a tool for conflict resolution in some criminal cases, particularly for serious violent crimes. In such cases, making the victim whole usually requires that the perpetrator suffer a greater hardship than restitutionary justice would typically provide.

Rehabilitation

The prominence of rehabilitation as an objective of criminal justice has been cyclical in nature. Even during my own thirty-year legal career, the emphasis on attempting to reform serious felons has dramatically ebbed and flowed. In the midst of significant growth in prison populations, social scientists, liberal academics and editorialists, and perceptive politicians tend to cry out for alternative sentences that emphasize treatment, education, and other self-improvement opportunities in lieu of incarceration. We need to address the root cause of crime, they say. But when crime rates are rising and research studies indicate that large expenditures for rehabilitation programs have failed to make a difference, law enforcement, conservative editorialists, and perceptive politicians are equally vociferous in clamoring for longer incarceration of offenders to achieve public safety. In the last two decades of the twentieth century, this latter group of advocates carried the day. Crime rates rose dramatically in the late 1970s and early 1980s. Congress and state legislatures responded with longer prison sentences and, more significantly, minimum mandatory sentences for many crimes. Prison populations grew dramatically on both the state and federal level. While critics of this policy shift allege it has been prohibitively expensive and has diverted funds from better uses, such as education and healthcare, proponents quickly point to the fairly dramatic decrease in crime rates that has followed.

Despite such cycles in which rehabilitation is emphasized or deemphasized, I believe that most people who work in the trenches of the criminal justice system understand that it's not an either-or proposition. In reality, at the same time as prison populations have grown, we have also been spending ever-increasing amounts on a variety of rehabilitation programs, both in and out of prison. We're also spending ever-increasing amounts on early-education programs designed to keep kids out of trouble. The problem is that many of our rehabilitation programs are not good investments. And we rarely have an effective means of evaluating them and abandoning them when appropriate. Based on my extensive experience, I believe the root cause of so much crime in the United States is family dysfunction, and too few rehabilitation programs adequately address the realities confronting people who have not had the benefit of proper parenting.

I'm not a complete pessimist. Some rehabilitation programs do work for some offenders. It depends upon the program, and it depends upon the offender. For minor juvenile offenders, a diversion program with minimal intervention that reinforces parental efforts to effect change will result in a high percentage of participants never re-offending. Alcohol education and therapy for an incipient drinker who gets a drunk-driving ticket may well solve the problem. Probation works for a considerable number of first-time offenders. Good mentoring programs that address the reality of ineffective parenting can save some young offenders. On the other hand, for highly recidivist offenders between the age of sixteen and thirty, most rehabilitation programs have low success rates. It's too late to rescue them from their antisocial bent.

I spent four years on the board of directors of a nonprofit community corrections program in Colorado Springs where offenders sentenced by the court went to work in the community during the day and returned to the facility at night to participate in various programs to address their deficiencies. Many offenders performed well under such supervision and never re-offended. But a significant percentage failed and wound up in prison. The single greatest factor in predicting success appeared to be the existence of a support group, usually family members, who genuinely cared whether the offender succeeded.

There's a lot of myths about who's in prison in the United States. Critics would have you believe our prisons are full of first-time, nonviolent offenders. In my experience, nothing could be further from the truth. Our state prisons are full of violent offenders and highly recidivist nonviolent offenders, with a handful of major white-collar criminals. Our federal prisons are full of drug dealers, violent offenders, and major white-collar criminals.

The Colorado prison system is instructive. When I ran the Colorado Department of Corrections from 1999 to 2001, there were approximately eighteen thousand inmates. As I analyzed the data from the department, about 75 percent were in prison for a violent offense, had committed a violent offense in the past, or were charged with a violent offense before plea bargaining to a nonviolent offense. The quarter of inmates who could truly be considered nonviolent offenders, who didn't pose a threat to the physical safety of other people, averaged almost three prior felonies apiece. A significant percentage of these nonviolent offenders hadn't been sentenced to prison initially for their current offense, but had failed on probation or community corrections. The prison population was 92 percent male, and 80 percent were under thirty at the time of their initial incarceration. Minorities were disproportionately represented. Half of the inmates hadn't graduated from high school or received a GED prior to their incarceration. Less than 2 percent were college graduates. But the most clearly defining characteristic of the prison population, more so than race or education, had to do with parentage. Fully two-thirds of all Colorado inmates, both men and women, had never at any point in their life lived with their natural father. Only 10 percent of the inmates lived with both their parents at the time of emancipation. The inmate population in Colorado was typical of state prison populations.

Most of these inmates didn't technically need rehabilitation. They needed *habilitation*. They needed to learn the basic values and life skills necessary to lead a crime-free life; things most people learn at home. Their lack of parenting had left many of them without empathy or an adequately developed conscience. They'd been sentenced to prison either because they committed a serious enough crime that the law required it, or because a judge, assessing their past record and current offense, deemed them a serious enough threat to the public safety to order them incarcerated.

Critics complain that the United States incarcerates a higher percentage of its population than other western industrialized countries, and some suggest it's a sign of penal barbarism. In fact, our high incarceration rates are explained by the fact that we have a very high rate of illegitimacy, of family dysfunction, and, consequently, a very high rate of violent crime.

Is it possible to be rehabilitated (or habilitated) in prison? As one who has managed a large prison system, my answer is that it is possible, but that hoped-for rehabilitation shouldn't be the primary reason for sending someone to prison. Retribution, isolation, and deterrence are better reasons for imprisonment. But many criminals sent to prison have lives spinning out of control, and time spent in prison can stop the downward spiral, at least temporarily. It allows the inmate to dry out from an addiction and restore some basic discipline to their life. Inmates in all but the most secure setting get out of bed each morning, go to work or school, eat meals at regular times, and go to bed at regular times. Good prison systems give strong incentives to inmates to get a high school education or perhaps more. A high school education significantly enhances their chances of succeeding upon release. Prison may also be an inmate's first exposure to any spiritual dimension in their life. Statistics show that the most successful rehab program in prison is also the least expensive—Alcoholics Anonymous. For a significant number of inmates, prison will be a "bottoming-out" experience. I'm aware of many genuine conversions that prison inmates have undergone.

Yet, prisons are full of criminals, and U.S. prisons are full of hard-core criminals. So, there aren't many good role models, and there's no question that young criminals can be hardened by the prison experience. Prison isn't the best setting for rehabilitation, but because of the need for public safety, it's oftentimes the only feasible one.

Isolation

Public safety is a very good reason to incarcerate someone. Throughout my career as a prosecutor, and before and after my tenure as a prison administrator, I have not been reluctant to argue vociferously that prisons "work." By that I mean they work well when it comes to isolating dangerous and recidivist criminals from the law-abiding public and thereby enhancing public safety. I firmly believe that the significant decline in crime rates in the 1990s was directly related to the increasing rates of incarceration that began in the second half of the 1980s. Incarcerating a highly recidivist young offender, who would otherwise commit as many as a hundred felonies per year, buys a great deal of public safety. Incarcerating him for a significant period of time will save many people from becoming his victims. It's also a fact of criminology that many types of offenders burn out with age. A habitual criminal sentenced to prison at twenty-two may re-offend when he's paroled at thirty-seven. But he's very likely to offend with less frequency and to become less violent with age. Rates of violent offenses decline dramatically in the over-thirty-five population. My hope is that criminal sentencing will become more scientific and take into account the criminological reality that inmates pose less of a danger with age. Once retribution and general deterrence is accomplished, there's no reason to have our prisons full of inmates over sixty years of age. There are exceptions, however. Pedophiles don't decrease their predatory activity until advanced age impacts their mobility and takes them out of contact with children. I have prosecuted pedophiles who were over eighty at the time of their offense. One was in a wheelchair and on oxygen. All too frequently, they have perpetrated on multiple generations of family members. Judges can rightly decide isolation in prison until death is the only acceptable alternative for them.

Deterrence

Deterrence is a universally accepted objective of criminal sentencing. People may argue whether a particular sentence achieves deterrence, but no one argues that deterrence should not be a goal of the criminal law. Legislatures set sentences and courts impose them to achieve both specific deterrence of the individual offender and general deterrence of the community that learns of its imposition.

It's axiomatic that in order to be deterred from an illegal act, a potential perpetrator must view the adverse consequences of getting caught as exceeding the benefits of committing the crime. But that equation is sometimes difficult to apply in the real world. Not all people are deterred to the same extent by the same possible consequence. Some offenders, particularly many young offenders, seem largely oblivious to the risks and rewards of crime. Depending on one's economic circumstances, the chance of getting caught may seem very low for certain activities, such as drug dealing, when the possible rewards seem comparatively high. And even if caught, some offenders, particularly young first-time nonviolent offenders, are aware that the chance of any significant punishment is relatively small. Nevertheless, for most of us, deterrence is a very important part of the law. The vast majority of Americans never commit a serious criminal offense precisely because they fear the consequences, both legal and nonlegal. The likelihood of severe punishment for the most severe crimes, such as murder, is more than sufficient to deter most people from ever seriously considering committing them.

I believe, despite the opposing view of many, that prison is a significant deterrent to crime. It's my observation that most people dread the prospect of going to prison and are less likely to commit an offense if they believe there's a reasonable likelihood they could wind up there. The more intelligent the person and the more invested they are in the community, the more deterrable they are. Accordingly, in my experience, white-collar crime is more susceptible to deterrence than street crime. In dysfunctional families, where prison has been a part of life for successive generations, the deterrent effect of the criminal law is, unfortunately, much more likely to be attenuated.

Minimum Mandatory Sentencing

When I first began prosecuting cases in 1977, Colorado had a system of indeterminate sentencing under which judges were given very broad discretion. An armed robber, for example, could receive a sentence ranging from probation to forty years in prison. Judges regularly utilized that broad discretion to impose widely variant and seemingly inconsistent sentences in accordance with their personal philosophical bent. Your fate as a convicted defendant was truly a matter of the luck of the draw.

In the mid-1980s, the Colorado legislature, like many others around the country, rebelled. In the wake of rising serious-crime rates and a corresponding public outcry, they instituted a system of determinant sentences and minimum mandatory sentences. By 1986, an armed robber in Colorado could be sentenced to a term of eight to sixteen years and was ineligible for probation. In other words, a sentence of at least eight years was mandatory. All violent criminals were exposed to such minimum mandatory sentences. The prison population in Colorado, and other states that instituted such a sentencing scheme, exploded in the ensuing years. And over the next fifteen years, the violent-crime rate also dropped significantly.

On the federal level, Congress imposed upon the courts a system of sentencing guidelines under which the United States Sentencing Commission, within a range prescribed by Congress, determined what sentences should be imposed on similarly situated defendants. The guidelines are extraordinarily detailed, and federal judges have had very little discretion in sentencing.

Most judges and defense attorneys decry sentencing guidelines and minimum mandatory sentences. At heart, I'm not a big fan of removing sentencing discretion from judges. I believe each case is somewhat unique and that judges should have the ability to react to the peculiarities of each case. So, in general, I would like to see greater discretion return to the sentencing function, and I believe that will be the trend in the near future.

But, as indicated above, I believe the judiciary brought the problem of greatly curtailed sentencing discretion upon themselves. When the courts had indeterminate sentencing options, I saw little or no effort by judges to pursue consistency and fairness by taking into account what other judges were doing. To the contrary, they jealously guarded the power of individual judges to be as arbitrary as they wanted to be in imposing their own philosophy of punishment. The resulting wide variations in sentencing were disturbing to the public and to their elected representatives. While judges should have independence and broad discretion to exercise their judicial functions, they cannot forget that the separation of powers makes the determination of what conduct is criminal, and what the possible penalties should be, the exclusive province of the legislative branch. Congress and state legislatures properly perceived a problem and acted to solve it. In doing so, they proved a point to the courts that I hope will not soon be forgotten.

I favor determinate sentencing and some mandatory minimum sentences in the most serious crimes as a means of checking unbridled and arbitrary discretion by judges. But it's my belief that Congress and the state legislatures should allow greater levels of judicial discretion to return to the sentencing function as a means of permitting judges to respond to the unique facts and circumstances present in each case. The less serious the case, the greater discretion should be allowed. The larger the defendant's criminal record, the less discretion should be permitted. I don't believe minimum mandatory sentences are necessary for first-time property crimes and for drug users and drug possessors. While judges have different philosophical approaches to such crimes, most of them are diligent and well-meaning and should be allowed to impose sentences they believe have the best chance to achieve the objectives of the criminal law. In short, there's an appropriate middle ground to be reached.

The Death Penalty

Although I authored a paper in college entitled *The Death Penalty: Cruel and Unusual or Just Unusual?* in which I generally supported the concept of the death penalty, I had no real-world experience with capital punishment at the time and no strong feelings about it. That changed with my role as an intern in the Colorado Springs District Attorney's Office in assisting the prosecution team in the death penalty cases of Michael Corbett and Freddie Lee Glenn, which I described in the first chapter. I came away from those cases believing that for the heinous murder of innocent victims, such as Karen Grammer, any penalty short of the death penalty would not reflect the abhorrence society had for the conduct and would demean the value of the victim's life. My subsequent experience over many years as a prosecutor, including all the opposition to the death penalty that I have encountered, has tended to strengthen my initial impressions. I remain convinced that in certain heinous cases, such as Timothy McVeigh's bombing of the federal building in Oklahoma City, or Ted Bundy's serial murders of young women, the death penalty is the most appropriate societal response. I also believe that in the age of terrorism and mass killings, the death penalty remains a viable and necessary option. But I also recognize my position is at odds with that of many intelligent people whose viewpoint I respect. As a Roman Catholic, my views about the death penalty are in opposition to the current view, although not the historical view, of the church hierarchy. Largely because of that, I've frequently been called upon to debate the issue in various forums and to explain my position.

In a free society, the people themselves, through their elected representatives, determine the provisions of the social contract. The people enact the criminal laws and determine what the consequences should be for the breach of such laws. This holds true for every offense from running a red light to first-degree murder. The punishment must be severe enough to deter the undesirable conduct and dissuade the victims from seeking revenge outside the terms of the social contract. To illustrate, murder is a social evil of such magnitude that the societal sanction cannot be a $50 fine. Many potential perpetrators would conclude that was a very small price to pay to get rid of a nemesis, and many loved ones of murder victims would be strongly inclined to take the law into their own hands in retaliation. The punishment must fit the crime.

Given the societal interests, it seems logical that the people, through their elected representatives, can conclude that the most severe possible punishment, death, is an appropriate sanction for the most heinous crimes. That was also the view of the Roman Catholic Church until relatively recently. In *Summa Theologica*, Thomas Acquinas wrote a compelling defense of the death penalty as a natural extension of the principle of self-defense. Only in the last several decades have the bishops of the church determined that, largely because of modern methods of incarceration, the death penalty is no longer necessary to promote public safety and that no other objective of the death penalty justifies its imposition. I have found pastoral letters on the subject to be thoughtful and well written, and I greatly respect the position taken by the Church, even though I disagree with the conclusion that the death penalty no longer implicates the principles of self-defense. When an inmate serving a life term kills a prison guard, or when a terrorist in prison directs another terrorist attack, isn't simply continuing to incarcerate them an inadequate societal response? We also have a growing problem with violent criminals facing long sentences directing their cohorts to kill the witnesses against them. Only the death penalty could be an adequate deterrent to such behavior, which is a terrible affront to our system of justice.

I have respect for those who hold a belief that the death penalty is immoral. While I personally have no trouble making a moral and ethical distinction between the murder of an innocent person that occurs with malice aforethought and contrary to the laws of society and the execution of a person who, after due process provided by a duly constituted authority, has been convicted of engaging in such an act, I accept that many others are not able to make that distinction and that my moral view may not be as fully developed as theirs.

I have less respect for courts, particularly appellate courts, that have engaged in intellectual dishonesty to undermine the will of the majority in regard to the death penalty and to impose their own moral view. The suggestion of some judges that the death penalty is cruel and unusual punishment violative of the Eighth Amendment is ludicrous to all but the most extreme living constitutionalists. There is a myriad of documentary evidence that shows the framers of the Constitution did not view death as cruel and unusual punishment for serious crimes. It was frequently imposed for such crimes, and they made no effort to halt the practice. Rather, they were concerned about various forms of torture, including decapitation of limbs, that had been used in response to property crimes. Capital punishment is referenced in the Constitution itself, and the fact that the framers prohibited the taking of one's life without due process indicates they were amenable to the execution of certain heinous criminals after due process.

As to the contention of living constitutionalists, such as Justices Brennan and Marshall, that the death penalty no longer comports with "society's evolving standards of decency," I find it elitist to suggest that unelected judges should make such a determination rather than the people themselves or their elected representatives. The voting citizens in many states indicate they are very much disposed toward executing heinous murderers. Interference by the courts with the will of the people should be based on genuine legal issues in a particular case and not on the fact that the legal intelligentsia has a different moral view.

By the same token, if and when the people decide that the death penalty, because of concerns about inconsistent application, evolving moral standards, or any other consideration, should be abandoned, then it should be. But it must be the people and not the courts that come to that conclusion.

It's my conclusion, after dealing with the issue for many years, that the public that sits on juries is unwilling to impose the death penalty with sufficient frequency and consistency to make it a highly effective general deterrent. I've seen juries fail to impose the penalty in the most heinous of cases, including one in which the defendant tracked down and executed all the innocent witnesses to the armed robbery of a convenience store so a cohort could not be successfully prosecuted for the robbery. The jury felt sorry for the defendant because of his troubled past. But I'm also convinced that if the death penalty were abandoned by every state, it would only be a matter of time before a heinous case, such as the Oklahoma City bombing case or another incident of terrorism, caused the public to seek its reinstatement.

Colorado abolished the death penalty in 1897 in response to a growing abolitionist movement. But in 1900, four inmates escaped from the Colorado State Penitentiary after stabbing a twenty-eight-year-old guard, William Rooney, to death. One of the four, Thomas Reynolds, was captured four days later outside of Cañon City. Instead of returning him to the prison, the citizens of Cañon City hung him from a light pole. Some newspapers in the state recognized the vigilante action as an appropriate protest to the abolition of capital punishment. The Colorado legislature reinstated the death penalty the next year.

Given the vehement opposition to the death penalty throughout the world and the ferocity of opponents in the United States, including the legal intelligentsia, I suspect there will be relatively few executions in the near term. For my part, I'll continue to examine my conscience concerning the issue, but I suspect I'll continue to view death as an appropriate punishment in a narrow class of particularly heinous murders that combine obvious premeditation and overwhelming evidence of guilt and for which any other penalty seems to me to be an inadequate societal response.

The Juvenile Justice System

Prior to 1900, there was no separate juvenile justice system in this country. Children above the age of reason were generally tried and punished the same as adults. While a few states had provisions for treating juveniles differently upon conviction, such as incarcerating them in separate facilities, there wasn't a separate court system until Chicago created one in 1899. But the concept then spread rapidly. The movement toward juvenile courts coincided with other child protection reforms, including the adoption of child labor laws. The adult criminal justice system was viewed as overly harsh, punitive, and formalistic, and there was deemed a need for more emphasis on nurturing, treatment, and rehabilitation for young offenders. By 1925 all but two states had a distinct juvenile justice system, and those two fell in line during the next two decades.

Juvenile courts were designed to be equity courts, characterized by flexibility, guardianship, and protection of the child without the rigidity and emphasis on retribution that characterized the adult courts. By original conception, the juvenile courts were designed to be less contentious and less adversarial. To underscore this philosophy, they adopted terms like *delinquent* rather than *criminal* and *adjudicate* rather than *convict*. The statutory purpose of the juvenile courts was almost always described as "the best interests of the child."

And so things proceeded without much controversy until 1967, when the U.S. Supreme Court decided the case of *In re Gault*. In that case, the Warren Court extended most of the constitutional protections of adult defendants to juveniles. While this was done for the noble purpose of correcting perceived abuses in what was sometimes viewed as an overly informal structure lacking due process, the result was to change the juvenile justice system dramatically. It lost much of its caretaker characteristics and became a more adversarial process. The delays that were common in the adult system became common in the juvenile system, with the result that the court lost much of its *parens patriae* (in the place of the parents) capabilities, because defense lawyers and jury trials are not, after all, the process by which effective parental discipline is customarily dispatched. We created a system in which a first-time juvenile burglar was often a tenth-time burglar by the time his original case was adjudicated. And we constructed a system where "the best interests of the child," at least in the eyes of the general public, became synonymous with minimizing consequences for the child.

The juvenile codes in all the states were fundamentally revised in the next few years after the *In re Gault* decision in 1967. And those codes remained largely intact well into the 1980s and early 1990s, despite significant changes in the demographics of violent crime. In Colorado our juvenile code provided for a maximum period of detention for a juvenile of two years. At the same time, we began to dramatically reduce the number of institutional beds in the state for juveniles and the mentally ill. By the mid-1980s, the state had only about 210 secure beds for juveniles that were under state direction and about another 130 under private contract. Meanwhile, the under-eighteen population had doubled in twenty years and the nature of juvenile crime had changed dramatically. Between 1967 and 1987, the per capita rate of violent crime committed by juveniles had tripled. The FBI crime index showed juveniles were committing 40 percent of all serious crimes. Because of the pressure on the few available beds, serious juvenile offenders in Colorado were routinely paroled in six months or less. We essentially had a system that was designed to deal with kids stealing hubcaps and vandalizing mailboxes that was now dealing with highly recidivist young offenders committing rape, robbery, and murder. Yet, we had no place to put them. And public safety suffered greatly.

When I was elected district attorney in Colorado Springs in 1988, I set juvenile justice reform as my number-one priority. While it took some time, by 1993 the state's twenty-two district attorneys had secured widespread support for the effort to overhaul the juvenile code. We were aided by the fact that the summer of 1993 was dubbed the "summer of violence" by the Colorado media because of so many juvenile homicides and assaults in Denver. As a consequence, the legislature gave prosecutors the discretion to direct file into the adult system any juvenile between fourteen and eighteen who had committed a violent felony. Further, the courts were given discretion to sentence a violent juvenile offender convicted in adult court to an adult sentence in an adult facility, or to a somewhat shorter sentence in a facility run by the Department of Corrections, which was designed solely for youthful violent offenders. Sentences to the Youth Offender System (YOS), as it was called, could range from two to seven years, with no parole eligibility. Those who failed in YOS could have the adult sentence imposed. The emphasis at YOS was on discipline and academic improvement. At intake, the young offenders spent months in a boot camp, breaking down their gang affiliations and instilling basic discipline in their lives. They then entered an academic program that led to a high school diploma, not a GED. College courses and vocational training were also available. Finally, the last six months of a sentence were spent in community reintegration.

While the demographics of all crime, including juvenile crime, are complex and difficult to analyze, the fact is that violent juvenile crime rates in Colorado have fallen dramatically since 1993, when serious consequences once again became a possibility for serious juvenile offenders.

I have come to the conclusion that an effective criminal justice system must be capable of dealing effectively with two fundamentally different groups of young offenders. A juvenile system should be retained to deal quickly and decisively with a large group of minor and incipient juvenile offenders to ensure that they are deterred from more-serious or chronic criminal involvement. There are numerous cases in our juvenile courts today that used to be dealt with outside the courts by effective parenting and communication with victims. When Johnny intentionally broke the neighbor's window or vandalized his mailbox, the neighbor didn't need to call the police because he was confident Johnny's parents would deal with the issue very effectively. Unfortunately, that's not always true today. Those types of court cases can typically be dealt with through a diversion program with meaningful contractual provisions and involving whatever parental support is available. More serious, but still incipient, offenders can be dealt with by a range of sanctions up to and including detention in a juvenile facility. There must be a high level of supervision and accountability.

But as to the other group of juvenile offenders, the young but hard-core violent offenders that are the greatest public safety threat on our streets, we must be willing to incapacitate them for long enough to make a difference for them and for the public's safety. For a seventeen-year-old who commits armed robbery or assault with a deadly weapon, retribution, deterrence, or isolation don't require us to throw away the key after a first offense. But you also cannot engender public respect for the law unless you deal with such offenders in a manner that sends a message about the unacceptability of such behavior, yet still provides a chance to avoid becoming a habitual violent offender. In my opinion, most juvenile courts don't have options that make them capable of reaching the proper balance for such serious juvenile offenders. An intermediate sanction, somewhere between adult prison and juvenile detention, is more appropriate.

V. A Higher Duty

Prosecutorial Politics and Ethics

You're a prosecutor, not a persecutor, and you need to understand and appreciate the difference.

A hotel maid was making her rounds cleaning guest rooms about 9:00 A.M. When she knocked on the door of one room, a male opened the door. Before she could say anything, the man grabbed her and pulled her into the room. He then proceeded to brutally rape her, tie her up, and gag her before leaving the room. Upon being discovered, the victim described the perpetrator and reported that she didn't see anyone else in the room.

The police learned the hotel room in question had been leased the night before by a woman they quickly determined was a prostitute. The prostitute told the police that when she left the room about 7:30 A.M., two males, whom she believed to be related, remained behind. She gave the police enough information for them to ascertain the identity of the two males. They were cousins, closely resembled each other, and had both served time in prison for sexual assault. Both also refused to be questioned by the police. A photo lineup was prepared by the police that included photos of the two suspects and three others. The victim picked out the photo of one of the cousins and he was arrested for the crime. But before the district attorney's office would file the case, we insisted that a live lineup be held. In that lineup, the victim picked out the other cousin.

We spent several days making exhaustive efforts to

determine which of the two men committed the offense. No physical evidence at the scene or on the victim was recovered. Failing to resolve the question, we released the man from custody and declined to file charges, despite the fact that we knew both men were convicted rapists and one of them had committed the crime. As district attorney, I met with the victim and her husband personally to explain our decision. She cried, and he expressed anger and frustration.

A difficult decision for a prosecutor? Not really. Given the law and the lack of evidence, any good prosecutor would reach the same result. Decisions of that nature are made every day by prosecutors, despite the understandable angst of victims and the criticism of the police, the media, and the public. The prosecutor knows the case will fail in court, and no amount of public pressure will make it otherwise. That's not to say public pressure never causes a prosecutor to file a case. The worst example I've seen is the prosecution of three Duke University lacrosse players by the district attorney in Durham, North Carolina. While the prosecutor was in the midst of a heated reelection race, an African American woman who worked as a stripper alleged she was raped at a Duke lacrosse team party. Durham has a large African American population, and activists were outraged and demanded justice be done. Despite the fact that no DNA or other physical evidence supported the allegation, that fellow strippers said the accuser was lying, and that the accuser had a history of psychological problems, including false reporting, the embattled DA filed the charges. He won the election, but the case quickly fell apart and the prosecutor lost his reputation, his job, and his license to practice law. He was properly subjected to discipline for withholding exculpatory evidence from the defendants. The system ultimately worked, but the accused paid a great price for the prosecutor's misconduct. Fortunately, such egregious cases are rare.

Sometimes the public pressure is *not* to prosecute. The decision to prosecute is met with media criticism and public outrage. The most severe editorial criticism I ever received was for charging a manager of a Christian boys ranch with child abuse. The ranch was operated by New Life Church, an evangelical megachurch in Colorado Springs, and its pastor, Ted Haggard, who was later the center of a well-publicized scandal. Evangelicals were infuriated by my decision and sent me hundreds of protest letters. I was ultimately proven right, but, not surprisingly, the local newspaper never acknowledged that fact. To his credit, Ted Haggard sent me a private letter apologizing for his public criticism of me.

Most of the heads of public prosecution offices in the United States are elected. Whether they're called attorney general, district attorney, state's attorney, county attorney, or county prosecutor, the person in charge of enforcement of the criminal laws of most states must periodically face the voters. The U.S. attorney general and the U.S. attorneys who enforce the criminal laws on the federal level are political appointees of the elected president of the United States. This circumstance would logically cause people to conclude that politics pervades the prosecution function. For the most part, they'd be wrong. Based on my experience as both an elected and a politically appointed prosecutor, I believe politics does play a role in prosecution, but not typically an unhealthy one.

It's my consistent observation that elected prosecutors tend to generally reflect the law enforcement philosophy of the constituents who elect them. For example, I can think of a few heinous murder cases that occurred in Boulder, Colorado, a liberal university town, for which the elected district attorney chose not to ask for the death penalty. In one case, a person in prison for murder escaped, went to Boulder, and executed two innocent people in a nearby campground. The Boulder community was undaunted by the prosecutor's failure to seek the death penalty, despite the fact that it clearly met the statutory criteria. He was easily reelected a year later. If the same case had occurred in my jurisdiction of Colorado Springs and I made the same decision not to seek the death penalty, I would have been tarred and feathered by the public, the media, and the police. I also believe community sentiment plays a significant role in how elected prosecutors establish their priorities. In the ski resort of Aspen, Colorado, drug cases have historically been a lower priority than they are in more conservative parts of the state.

Recognizing these realities about the role of politics in prosecution, I nevertheless support the popular election of most state and local prosecutors. As I'll discuss in a subsequent chapter, I have some reservations about the election of state attorneys general, but that doesn't stem from their role in prosecuting traditional crimes. I believe periodic political elections and campaigns bring appropriate public accountability to the prosecution function. Candidates must articulate their experience, their philosophy, and their priorities. More importantly, the election of prosecutors provides an important opportunity for the public to have some participation in and influence on the criminal justice system. One of the main reasons I favor popular election of prosecutors is because I do not favor popular election of judges. Unlike prosecutors, judges are not advocates. They're fact finders and neutral arbiters of the law. To be truly independent, as judges should be, they must be free from the vicissitudes of the campaign trail and the ever-fluctuating whims of the electoral majority. I do, however, favor periodic retention elections for judges (in which voters are asked whether they want to retain a judge) with public recommendations by a judicial performance commission as a means of some public accountability. The lifetime tenure of federal judges, with no mechanism for accountability other than impeachment, makes them more than independent. It makes too many of them arrogant and insufferable. Retention elections for judges appointed by an elected chief executive is, in my opinion, a fair balance between judicial independence and judicial accountability. And where judges are not elected, the election of prosecutors is all the more important as a direct means for the public to influence the priorities of criminal justice. I believe it's vital we retain that ability.

In some prosecution offices, particularly small ones, there can be considerable turnover in personnel when a new prosecutor is elected. That in itself is not necessarily a bad thing. Prosecutors should have enough control over personnel in their office to effectuate the changes, if any, they want to accomplish. In prosecution offices of any size, the turnover rate after an election is typically low. The professional staff in the office generally views the mission of the office as more important than the political leanings of the current boss, and the new boss needs the expertise of the professional staff. Most postelection turnover in large offices tends to occur at high managerial levels. When I was elected district attorney and took over an office of 160 people, I only asked three to leave, including the top assistant and two nonlawyer program heads who were political appointees of my predecessor. When I first became Colorado attorney general, none of my 350 employees were asked to leave.

The environment in a public prosecution office is such that the lawyers very frequently develop a foxhole mentality in which loyalty transcends politics. They intimately share with each other the thrill of victory and the agony of defeat. This tends to engender a high level of loyalty to one another and to a leader who genuinely appreciates their efforts. When I became the presidentially appointed U.S. attorney in Colorado, with the support of the state's two Republican senators, my predecessor as U.S. attorney became the Democratic Party's nominee to oppose one of the incumbent Senators. To the chagrin of the incumbent senator, some of the Republican lawyers in my office contributed to the Senate campaign of their former boss. The senator and his staff couldn't understand why they'd done so, but I did. Their loyalty, based on their bond as prosecutors, transcended politics. And they quickly developed the same loyalty to me. Many of the Democratic lawyers who have worked for me through the years enthusiastically contributed to my campaign for attorney general.

While politics plays a role in how prosecutors set their priorities and conform their law enforcement philosophy to their constituency, in my career I have observed remarkably little politics in the routine day-to-day decision making in the offices I was associated with and surprisingly little politics in the work of associations of prosecutors to which I belonged. A successful prosecution requires sufficient evidence that a specific criminal statute has been violated. When the case proceeds to court, the prosecutor must be prepared to prove it beyond a reasonable doubt. Politics cannot change the law or the evidence in a particular case. Reasonable and responsible prosecutors don't file charges that they believe are likely to be dismissed by the court prior to trial. Nor do they allow a grand jury to indict a suspect if the evidence is so insufficient that the prosecution will be embarrassed by subsequent rulings of the court. Defense attorneys like to say that prosecutors could persuade a grand jury "to indict a ham sandwich." But my response has always been, "But why would they?" You can't convict a ham sandwich at trial. Ultimately, as in the case of the DA from Durham, North Carolina, a prosecutor who brings politically motivated charges will pay a high price for it.

The modern criminal justice system has many checks and balances. The police investigate the allegations of citizens and can find evidence that either corroborates or disproves them. Prosecutors review the investigations of the police and determine whether charges are merited. Arrests require probable cause to believe the suspect has committed a crime and a court must confirm the existence of probable cause for a suspect to be detained before trial and as a precondition of the case proceeding to trial. In any case in which incarceration is a possible punishment, the defendant has a right to have a jury determine whether the government has proven its case beyond a reasonable doubt. Any alleged errors of the trial court can be appealed as of right. In such a system, prosecutorial decisions that are politically motivated and not adequately based on the law and the evidence are quickly exposed. A prosecutor can't bluff his way through a criminal case.

Sometimes, particularly in the federal system or in states where every felony case is presented to a grand jury, the prosecutor acts as a check to a whimsical grand jury, refusing to indict someone the grand jury wants to indict, because the prosecutor believes the evidence is insufficient to proceed to trial. That happened in a case in Colorado in which a grand jury wanted to indict individual employees of the Rocky Flats Plant for environmental crimes. But the U.S. attorney refused to indict them, striking a plea bargain with the corporate operator instead. The grand jurors were furious, believing the prosecutor had acted improperly. But the law is clear. An indictment requires the acquiescence of both the grand jury and the prosecutor.

I can't speak for the integrity of the justice system in every state. But I can assert that Colorado has a history of highly professional prosecution and a competent and effective public defender system. In combination with merit selection of judges, that promotes a criminal justice system as free of undesirable political influence as possible.

One reason for the professionalism of prosecution in Colorado has been the Colorado District Attorneys' Council. The statutorily recognized body has a full-time staff that arranges training for new prosecutors and continuing education for all prosecutors, applies for various training and program grants, and lobbies for or against proposed criminal law legislation. It has been a very effective organization. The elected district attorneys meet monthly to conduct the business of the council.

I have attended the meetings of the council for fifteen years as a local, state, and federal prosecutor. During the entire time, the political composition of the group was roughly half Democrat and half Republican. Until very recently, I wasn't aware of any instance in which the political diversity of the group impacted the nature and scope of its work. Only when voter-approved term limits for DAs went into effect in 2004, eliminating any seniority and mentoring among the district attorneys, have I seen them struggle to stay wholly apolitical. Some of the district attorneys were more professional and more effective than others, but that reality was wholly unrelated to political considerations. I heard concerns by district attorneys about the political ramifications of proposed legislation or the possible political fallout for them of a particular court decision or verdict, but I never heard any discussion about whether a case should be pursued or not pursued because of political implications. That's not to say individual prosecutors didn't contemplate such implications. But the focus of discussions was on the law or the evidence and on "doing justice," as prosecutors like to say.

I found pretty much the same mentality among my fellow U.S. attorneys. In fact, I was pleasantly surprised to find how many of the George W. Bush appointees had extensive prosecution backgrounds. That's not always the case. Even in the period immediately after the terrorist attacks of September 11, when the ACLU and some media were critical of John Ashcroft's administration of the Department of Justice, alleging that it was overzealous in pursuing national security, the communications from Ashcroft and the Department of Justice to the U.S. attorneys and among the U.S. attorneys themselves were devoid of political considerations. However, two years after my tenure as U.S. attorney ended, while Alberto Gonzales was U.S. attorney general, several of my former colleagues were removed from their positions, and it was suggested at Congressional hearings that political motivations were involved. Regardless of the merits of the matter, it was clear to me that the dismissals were poorly handled by the Justice Department. Given the traditions of the department, that was a very disappointing development.

While the job of state attorney general would, as described in a subsequent chapter, prove to be more political than my prior prosecutorial undertakings, I never heard political motives articulated by my attorney general colleagues as the basis for a prosecution, and the National Association of Attorneys General always attempted to articulate its collective view in a nonpartisan manner.

Despite my favorable experiences, there's no escaping the fact that most prosecutors are, by the nature of their job, charged with carrying out three seemingly conflicting roles: politician, advocate for the public, and administrator of justice. Simultaneously playing such roles is not easy and not recommended for the faint of heart or weak in character.

Professional Ethics

Much has been written and spoken about prosecutorial ethics, but not much of it has been authored by prosecutors.

As a result, much of the discussion has been in a negative vein. Defense attorneys, other advocates of accused persons, journalists, and legal disciplinary authorities are quick to publicize breaches of ethics by prosecutors. Frankly, I don't blame them. Few things are more pernicious than a rogue cop or an unethical prosecutor. I literally get sick to my stomach when I hear accounts of knowingly wrongful conduct by someone who takes an oath to uphold the constitutional rights of citizens.

Having said that, I've spent ten years in private practice and eighteen years as a prosecutor, and I will unequivocally assert that the level of ethical concern and compliance among the prosecutors I have associated with was higher than what I observed among private practitioners. Knowledgeable observers may find that faint praise. The fact is that prosecutors, because of their unique role in criminal justice as an advocate for the general public and not an individual client, have a higher ethical duty in many respects than other lawyers. Courts and disciplinary authorities have consistently recognized that higher duty. The prosecutor's responsibility goes beyond zealous advocacy for a client. Their responsibility is to pursue a just result, not merely to win cases. The following quote from Justice George Sutherland in a 1935 U.S. Supreme Court case eloquently describes the prosecutor's obligations within the criminal justice system:

> The [prosecutor] is the representative not of an ordinary party to a controversy, but of a sovereignty whose obligation to govern impartially is as compelling as its obligation to govern at all; and whose interest, therefore, in a criminal prosecution is not that it shall win a case, but that justice shall be done. As such, he is in a peculiar and very definite sense the servant of the law, the twofold aim of which is that guilt shall not escape or innocence suffer.

He may prosecute with earnestness and vigor—indeed, he should do so. But, while he may strike hard blows, he is not at liberty to strike foul ones. It is as much his duty to refrain from improper methods calculated to produce a wrongful conviction as it is to use every legitimate means to bring about a just one.[*]

Most state legal disciplinary agencies report that the number of grievances against prosecutors that are sustained constitute a comparatively low percentage of all unethical conduct by lawyers. In my career as a prosecutor, I've been the subject of several grievances filed by criminal defendants and one by a public defender. None was sustained. I believe that experience is very common among prosecutors. Angry defendants cooling their heels in prison are the source of the greatest number of complaints.

Based on my observations, the greatest ethical area of concern, especially for young prosecutors, and the one that's most apt to generate a sustainable complaint is the obligation to ensure that any potentially exculpatory or mitigating evidence is provided to the defense. Prosecutors have both an ethical and constitutional responsibility to disclose the existence of evidence known to the prosecutor that is favorable to the accused and is material to the issues of guilt or proper punishment.

Another common problem area is contact with a represented party without consulting his attorney. This can be a particularly sticky issue when the accused initiates the contact and says he doesn't want his lawyer involved.

Finally, the most publicized ethical cases involving prosecutors have included situations where the apprehension of a very dangerous suspect or location of a kidnap victim or victim's body is at stake and the prosecutor

---

[*] *Berger v. United States*, 295 U.S. 78, 88 (1935).

makes a very difficult decision that is second-guessed by the disciplinary authorities. The prosecutor engages in some form of deceit to secure the suspect's surrender or convince him to reveal the whereabouts of a victim. In such instances, it's not unusual for the public to sympathize with the prosecutor.

For private practitioners who breach ethical rules, the motive is often greed. They want to make more money. For prosecutors who violate ethical constraints, the motive is almost always a desire to win their case. It is unprofessional conduct for a prosecutor to charge or seek an indictment of a person on less than probable cause. As indicated earlier, given the checks and balances of the criminal justice system, it's also stupid to do so. It's possible for a prosecutor to have a malicious motive and seek to convict a defendant that the prosecutor has reason to believe is innocent, but such misconduct is extremely rare. The prosecutorial corruption that's more prevalent occurs precisely because the prosecutor is absolutely convinced of the defendant's guilt and neglects an ethical responsibility in order to make a conviction more likely. The strong belief in a defendant's guilt and the desire to hold him accountable creates a temptation to tolerate what he has reason to know is deceptive testimony by a witness, even if the witness is a police officer. Taking the witness to task for his deception by refusing to allow his testimony or by reporting the deception to the court will complicate an otherwise solid case. But an ethical prosecutor understands that their obligation to the integrity of the system surpasses their role as an advocate and does not tolerate any such corruption of the system.

What does all this say about the type of person who makes an ideal prosecutor? As a district attorney, U.S. attorney, and attorney general who has reviewed literally thousands of resumes and interviewed several hundred lawyer applicants, I've developed some fairly reliable criteria that I look for in a man or woman who wants to be a prosecutor. They have to be intelligent. You don't have to be brilliant to be a good prosecutor, but you have to be smart enough to conquer the intellectual challenges of the law and to write and argue your points clearly and effectively. As a general proposition, the academic credentials and experience level of those who apply for entry-level assistant U.S. attorney positions are superior to those who apply for entry-level deputy district attorney and assistant attorney general positions. That's largely a function of a better federal pay scale and the relative prestige of assistant U.S. attorney positions. Consequently, it's somewhat more difficult to identify future stars among the district attorney's office and attorney general's office applicant pools. But I'm proud of my success rate.

In addition, all prosecutors have to be excellent verbal communicators. Only such people will be successful in front of juries and judges. You must have the kind of personality that the trier of fact will find appealing, believable, and convincing. That typically also requires a genuinely cordial and professional demeanor. I will always recall a judge describing a young, struggling prosecutor in my DA's office as having a personality that "exudes reasonable doubt." His days as a trial lawyer were predictably short-lived.

But finally, and of very high importance, I look for people who have a sense of righteousness, who have a very well-developed and largely uncompromising sense of right and wrong. Righteousness has acquired bad connotations in our laid-back, anything-goes culture, but it's a great virtue. Only self-righteousness is a vice. Thomas Jefferson referred to righteousness as "rigid integrity" and said it was the first and foremost qualification in any profession. A righteous person has sufficient integrity to understand when the end doesn't justify the means. Only if prosecutors are sufficiently righteous can you be assured they will aggressively pursue the guilty but also never compromise the integrity of the process to reach a desired result.

When I was a young prosecutor, a defense attorney, angry that I wasn't making a better plea offer, mockingly yelled at me, "Suthers, you'd arrest your own mother!" With little hesitation or reflection, I responded, "Not unless there was probable cause to believe she'd committed a crime!" Word of the humorous exchange spread around the courthouse. My supporters have cited it to call me righteous. My detractors have cited it to call me a variety of other things.

The thing you *don't* want in a prosecutor, or anyone in law enforcement, for that matter, is someone trying to compensate for an inferiority complex by seeking a position that exercises power and control over other people. Almost everyone has encountered security personnel whose view of their own importance exceeds that set forth in their job description and who seem to take too much delight in ordering people around. I'm always alert to the possibility that an applicant is seeking a power trip and ask several questions designed to expose that propensity. As I have often told groups of young prosecutors, "You're a prosecutor, not a persecutor, and you need to understand and appreciate the difference." Or as Bill Ritter, the former Denver DA and governor of Colorado, was fond of saying, "If the only tool in your toolbox is a hammer, everything around you looks like a nail."

I've also found that good prosecutors have respect for and appreciate the importance of the criminal defense function. They understand the ethics of criminal defense and the reality that the defense attorney is constitutionally entitled to put the government to its proof, regardless of how despicable the crime and the person who committed it. They also understand when those ethics are violated. Good prosecutors and good defense attorneys understand each other, respect each other, and, in my opinion, should be capable of cordial professional relationships with each other.

I indicated earlier that the state public defender's office in Colorado is competent and effective. So I was always somewhat mystified and disappointed as a state prosecutor about the very antagonistic relationship that generally existed between the offices of the state's public defenders and the state's prosecutors. I once saw a written memorandum issued by the head of the public defender's office prohibiting his employees from socializing with prosecutors after hours, including Christmas parties, retirement parties, and so forth. Largely because Colorado had a death penalty, the public defender took the view that prosecutors were trying to kill their clients and every action or tactic was justified if it was done to undermine the prosecution's efforts. "Death is different" was their constant refrain. At their training seminars, they had sessions on guerilla tactics and how to create reversible error. In general, it appeared the Colorado Public Defender's Office took pride in operating outside the legal establishment. You never saw them at bar association functions or legal education programs. The public defenders whose courtroom behavior was the most questionable were the most heralded. Any friendliness with prosecutors was viewed as consorting with the enemy.

I had come to the reluctant conclusion that such antagonism was inherent in the prosecutor–public defender relationship—until I became U.S. attorney and learned otherwise. The Federal Public Defender's Office in Colorado was highly professional, highly competent, and highly ethical. Both the U.S. attorney's office and federal public defender's office had outstanding litigators who fought aggressively in court but maintained professional relationships both in and out of court. It made me realize the antagonism that was pervasive at the state level was not inherent in the relationship. Rather, I now believe it was a function of a longstanding culture created by some of the admired early pioneers of the state public defender's system. Their successors were promoted and then promoted others precisely because they accepted that culture and considered it important to perpetuate it.

Plea Bargaining

When elected prosecutors encounter political trouble, more often than not the problem stems from controversial plea bargains. Plea bargaining is as old as criminal justice itself, but it has become an increasingly integral part of the prosecution function as courts have been required to take on ever-larger caseloads. Yet, it remains a process that is largely misunderstood by the public. And I've found that a surprisingly large number of elected prosecutors aren't willing or aren't able to effectively communicate with their constituents about it. If they don't learn to do so quickly, their tenure in office is likely to be brief.

Nationwide, well over 90 percent of criminal cases don't proceed to trial. Urban courts would typically have trials in only 2 to 6 percent of cases. A small percentage of cases are completely dismissed after being charged because of insufficient evidence; the rest are disposed of by a guilty plea to one or more counts. Overall, a conviction rate of at least 85 to 90 percent (meaning 85 to 90 percent of all cases filed result in a guilty plea or conviction at trial) would be typical of a competent prosecutor's office. Almost all the guilty pleas result from a plea bargain. It's a bargain because the prosecution gives up something in consideration for the defendant's agreement to plead guilty. But contrary to the impression of so many unfamiliar with the inner workings of the criminal justice system, almost all plea bargains involve a legitimate and often significant benefit to the government. Professional ethics and disciplinary authorities have long since recognized the necessity and the benefit of plea bargaining. Exactly what factors drive a plea bargain vary greatly depending on the nature of the court and the seriousness of the charge.

In overburdened traffic and misdemeanor courts, plea bargains are a matter of survival. When I was district attorney in Colorado Springs, eight judges in the County Court handled forty thousand misdemeanor and serious traffic offenses each year. That meant every judge had to dispose of an average of fifty cases each day the courts were open. But they also had thousands of civil cases to handle. If all forty thousand cases went to trial, it would require approximately one hundred divisions of the court to handle them. Neither politicians nor taxpayers have shown themselves willing to finance such a system. In such overcrowded urban courts, prosecutors must establish guidelines that prioritize which cases should proceed to trial and which should be the subject of a standard plea offer. In drunk-driving cases, for example, a blood alcohol level of .10 was necessary to prove driving under the influence (DUI). (It has since been lowered by the legislature to .08). But we would routinely offer a plea bargain allowing the defendant to plead guilty to the lesser included offense of driving while ability impaired (DWAI) if the defendant had a blood alcohol level (BA) of less than .20, had not been involved in an accident, and had no prior alcohol-related conviction. For repeat offenders, those with BAs above .20, or those who had caused property damage, we would insist on a plea to DUI or proceed to trial. The legislature recognized the necessity of plea bargains in enacting penalties and administrative sanctions for drunk driving. All defendants convicted of either DUI or DWAI were sentenced to alcohol education and treatment. Those with previous alcohol-related records got jail time. Everyone with a BA over .10 lost their license through an administrative proceeding. Those who got convicted of DUI got a longer suspension. Similar sorts of guidelines were employed in disposing of other frequently occurring offenses. Only through such carrot-and-stick plea bargaining policies could courts avoid collapsing from case congestion.

For new prosecutors who operate in the high-volume traffic and misdemeanor courts, plea bargaining is an art form requiring patience, persuasion, creativity, and quick thinking. Disposing of up to a hundred cases per day leaves little time for extended negotiation. I distinctly recall my most creative plea bargain during my tenure in the misdemeanor courts. A man who had recently undergone bladder surgery stayed in the car in the parking lot while his wife went into a grocery store. She took longer than expected, and the man, feeling a strong need to relieve himself, did so behind a nearby Salvation Army drop-off bin. Unfortunately for him, he was seen by two elderly ladies who were appalled by his behavior. They called the police and insisted he be issued a citation for indecent exposure. When they all showed up for court, I quickly assessed the problem, despite my inexperience. I couldn't convict the man of indecent exposure, which required a sexual motive on his part. But the elderly women were adamant that this behavior not be tolerated. After perusing the statute book, I came up with an ingenious solution acceptable to all concerned. The defendant pled guilty to an amended charge of littering, acknowledging that he deposited "a foreign substance" on the ground, and paid a small fine. The ladies felt vindicated.

Because many defendants in misdemeanor and traffic cases are pro se, meaning they are representing themselves, humorous incidents are not uncommon. Flirtatious women will try to charm their way into a deal, and both men and women will dream up some outrageous but creative stories to explain their indiscretions. One man charged with indecent exposure claimed the woman who called the police was mistaken. It was not an exposed body part she saw, but rather a banana he was peeling in his lap. He didn't explain why he was sitting naked in his car while peeling a banana. I also recall a woman charged with drunk driving claiming she was stone sober when the accident happened, but that she had drank half a bottle of whiskey to relieve the stress before the police showed up.

In urban felony courts, the high volume of cases is, unfortunately, oftentimes a factor in the disposition of frequently occurring crimes like theft and burglary. In the courts of our largest cities, continued functioning of the court depends upon plea bargaining in a wide variety of felony cases. Once again, prosecutor's offices can only deal with such caseloads by establishing plea-bargaining guidelines that prioritize the most serious crimes that deserve the most serious consequences. Very often the plea bargain by the government involves a concession that is less of a bargain than it might appear. Prosecutors may dismiss multiple counts for a plea to one count, knowing full well that a conviction on all counts would not increase the sentence. Or the prosecution may agree to stipulate to a particular sentence in exchange for a plea of guilty, knowing full well that the judge is very unlikely to impose a sentence more harsh than the stipulated one, but also recognizing that the defendant doesn't want to take the minimal risk that he might. Good prosecutors and good defense attorneys know what judges are likely to do in the case of a conviction at trial and can intelligently advise victims and defendants about the risks and rewards of a proposed plea bargain.

Plea bargains in the most serious cases, such as rape, aggravated assault, murder, and the most egregious financial crimes, should, because of prioritization, be the least driven by docket congestion. That's not to say that even zealous prosecutors will not consider the dedication of resources required to prosecute a major case and take such considerations into account in analyzing plea offers by the defense. But good prosecutors handling such major cases will focus first and foremost on the strength of the evidence and the likelihood of conviction of the highest charge in evaluating whether to pursue a plea bargain. In a first-degree murder case, for example, a prosecutor will attempt to evaluate the chance of an acquittal, as well as the chance of a conviction of a lesser offense of second-degree murder or manslaughter, in formulating his strategy. If the case is seen by the prosecutor as rock-solid, a trial in the first-degree murder case is very likely. If premeditation will be a significant issue for the jury and there's a significant chance of a conviction of a lesser offense, perhaps even manslaughter, then a plea of second-degree murder may be viewed as a good plea bargain. It may also depend on the length of sentence the defendant is likely to get if convicted of the possible lesser offenses and the sentence that the prosecutor and defendant, respectively, are willing to accept.

Some plea bargains are necessary to procure a defendant's cooperation, typically his testimony against a codefendant. In serious cases, this requires a thorough and thoughtful analysis by the prosecution of the possible consequences. You need to make sure you're giving the deal to the right person, usually the least culpable. It may well be that the jury in the codefendant's trial will pass judgment on the wisdom of the plea bargain. If they believe the deal was too lenient, that may affect their view of the cooperating defendant's credibility. Decisions about which defendants to "turn" are difficult ones. Plea bargaining is not a science, it's an art form.

A specific case, which I consider one of the best plea bargains I ever struck, illustrates the quid pro quo and risk-and-reward analysis involved in a very high-profile murder case. Robert Sickich was a drug dealer. An undercover narcotics agent had made a purchase of cocaine from him at his mobile home one afternoon. The agent saw evidence that drugs were being stored and packaged for distribution in the home. The police secured a no-knock search warrant for the property and an arrest warrant for Sickich. When the warrants were executed that night, the law enforcement officers yelled, "Police, you're under arrest!" before smashing in the front door. Sickich was at the kitchen table dividing up and packaging cocaine. It took several seconds to smash in the door. Sickich shot and killed the first officer to enter the residence before being shot and paralyzed by the police. Sickich, whose prior record included drug offenses, was charged with first-degree murder, and my district attorney's office undertook consideration of whether it was appropriate to seek the death penalty. The killing of a law enforcement officer was an aggravating factor under Colorado law, which made a first-degree murder case eligible for the death penalty. The defense attorney for Sickich immediately indicated what his defense would be. Colorado had a "make my day" law that gave a homeowner the right to shoot any person he reasonably believed to be an unlawful intruder. Sickich would claim at trial he didn't hear anyone yell, "Police, you're under arrest!" Rather, he heard someone smashing in the front door, believed it to be an unlawful intruder, retrieved a gun from his bedroom, and shot the intruder. Because of the SWAT gear worn by the police, he didn't recognize them as law enforcement officers until it was too late. His planned defense set up an all-or-nothing proposition under Colorado law. Unless the prosecution could prove beyond a reasonable doubt that Sickich heard the officers yell "police" and could not reasonably believe an intruder was entering his residence, the jury would be instructed that they should acquit him on the murder charge. If the prosecution convinced the jury that Sickich knew it was the police executing a warrant, it was clearly a first-degree murder case. When the defense offered to plead guilty to first-degree murder and receive a life sentence without parole in exchange for the prosecution agreeing not to seek the death penalty, I quickly consulted the deceased officer's family and accepted the deal. The paralyzed Sickich spent about ten years in a prison hospital bed before he died—probably sooner than he would have if he had been given the death penalty.

There's no question that some bad plea bargains are struck in serious cases. I've seen some. Some prosecutors, because of inexperience or lack of resolve, may accept a plea bargain that doesn't reflect an intelligent analysis of the risks and rewards in a case and, therefore, does not promote the public interest. It's when a prosecutor cannot adequately explain to the public why a plea bargain in a high-profile case promotes the public interest that they tend to get into political trouble and words like *controversial* and *embattled* became associated with their name. Good prosecutors can explain the risks and rewards of a case and the benefits of a plea bargain in an ethical and appropriate manner after the deal is struck.

But, in my experience, there's one aspect of the risk analysis that prosecutors may not want to be too candid about. Given the random makeup of our juries, jury trials are inherently unpredictable. In some communities, the risk of getting jurors antagonistic to the government is greater than others. Prosecutors are very mindful of that reality. I knew one elected prosecutor who, when asked why he plea bargained a case, would typically candidly respond, "Because a jury was going to decide it." His candor was not rewarded by the electorate when he sought a second term.

The complexities of the U.S. legal system also add greatly to the risks of trial. Suppression of evidence, bad evidentiary rulings, and mistrials are always a possibility the prosecution must factor into its risk analysis. Add to that the possibility of reversible error occurring, which causes an appellate court to require the case to be retried.

So it's the high volume of cases, the investment in resources required for a jury trial, and the unpredictability of the result that combine to make plea bargains an attractive consideration for prosecutors and defendants alike. But what constitutes a good plea bargain, one that's in the public interest, involves a multitude of factors individual to a particular case.

Special Prosecutors

There's one aspect of prosecution that I believe has been inappropriately tarnished by politics: the role of the special prosecutor, or independent counsel, particularly on the federal level. In the aftermath of the Watergate scandal in the 1970s, Congress passed an independent counsel statute that was finally repealed in the aftermath of the Clinton impeachment hearings. The law resulted in the Department of Justice deferring to a special prosecutor in several situations in which no actual conflict of interest was identified but it simply looked bad for the Department of Justice to be investigating members of the same administration. The unseemly result over the intervening two decades was what some commentators have described as "politics by other means." The political party out of power at the White House attempted to use the independent counsel law to accomplish in court, or at least in the court of public opinion, what it had not accomplished at the ballot box. Anytime the out-of-power party secured the appointment of an independent prosecutor to investigate the presidential administration, the politics of scandal quickly took over. A long, drawn-out, and expensive investigation always brought about constant leaks and sensational headlines, regardless of what tangible results were achieved in court. The Iran Contra and Whitewater investigations were cases in point and evidence that both parties were guilty of exploiting the law. Unfortunately, the culture of the independent counsel law seems to have survived its repeal. Politicians still clamor for special prosecutors to investigate every allegation against members of the opposite party, often without articulating a legally recognizable conflict.

Special prosecutors are sometimes necessary, and courts should be empowered to finally determine the issue when there is a disagreement. A special prosecutor serves an important role on both the federal and state level by giving the public confidence that a case is being investigated and prosecuted by someone who doesn't have a personal or financial interest in its outcome.

I was appointed special prosecutor in a major corruption case involving two officers of the Denver Police Department. The officers were recruiting criminals with long records to plan burglaries and robberies. They would, in turn, recruit other hard-core criminals to commit the crime. The police informant was the wheel man and would drop off the other criminals at the crime scene and, unbeknownst to them, take off. The cops would then descend on the scene and catch the crooks in the act. They were dubbed the "super cops" because, more often than not, television cameras would be rolling when they made the bust. When the scheme unraveled, the affected district attorneys' offices were required to recuse themselves because the case impacted many of their pending prosecutions and they therefore had an apparent conflict of interest. My special prosecution was difficult because the best witness we had, one of the police recruits, had seven prior felony convictions. But justice prevailed.

My office was recused from another corruption case involving embezzlement from the county pension fund. Over my objection, the court ruled my office had a conflict because my deputies contributed to the pension fund. The Denver District Attorney's Office took over, and the embezzler got sixteen years in prison.

Special prosecutors should only be requested and appointed when actual conflicts and applicable ethical guidelines require it. Good prosecutors do their job regardless of who the suspect or the victim is, and history is replete with examples of outstanding work by prosecutors exposing public corruption on the part of former political allies or associates. In Colorado, it's not a conflict of interest to prosecute a former political contributor or supporter, and I can think of several instances in which I have charged former supporters of mine with crimes. A few wound up serving time in prison to ponder whether their support of me had been ill-advised. Prosecutors lose friends. It comes with the territory.

Victims' Rights and Criminal Justice Interest Groups

When I reflect back on the beginning of my legal career in 1977, it's easy for me to identify the aspect of the criminal justice system that has improved the most since then—the treatment of victims and witnesses. In 1977 most prosecution offices didn't have victim-witness units or any of the other programs that presently exist to assist the victims of crime to cope with their victimization and the ordeal of prosecuting their case. Many nonlawyers don't understand why it is that the victim of a crime is not a party to a criminal case and doesn't have the ability to control its prosecution. They don't fully comprehend that a criminal case is brought on behalf of all the people whose laws were violated and that sometimes interests other than an individual victim's interests are at stake. But they do understand something that it took way too long for people in the justice system to fully recognize: the protection of victims is why the system exists. As I've emphasized before, the government pursues justice on the victims' behalf because it doesn't allow victims to pursue it on their own. There's no excuse for not treating the victims of crime, even those who are not as innocent as we'd like, with dignity, respect, and compassion. The creation of victim compensation programs, restitution programs, and victim support resources was way overdue. Passage of Victims' Bill of Rights legislation has been generally positive. Today, there are many very dedicated victim advocates working in the criminal justice system, and they do an excellent job of educating victims on how the system works and getting them help to deal with the impact of crime.

Unfortunately, the increased emphasis on victims' rights has come at the same time as decreasing public confidence in our criminal justice system as a reliable fact-finding system. What victims of crime deserve more than anything else is a trial system that convicts the guilty with a high degree of consistency and makes wise use of limited judicial resources. On that score, the system too often fails the victims of crime.

The long-overdue emphasis on the interests of crime victims has spawned the growing influence of organizations formed to advocate for victims. While they have accomplished a great deal of good, on occasion I have had concerns about their tactics and the potential for some criminal justice interest groups to ignore the constitutional realities underpinning criminal justice. Some have not been content to advance the interests of victims, but rather assert that accused persons have "too many rights" without acknowledging that most such rights stem from the Bill of Rights, a document clearly designed by its framers to protect the rights of individuals, including accused individuals, vis-à-vis the state.

I've also seen a proliferation of defendant advocacy groups, particularly inmate advocacy groups. When I was director of corrections in Colorado, I met with inmate advocacy groups once per quarter to discuss their various concerns. While most of their concerns were legitimate, there were humorous expressions of naiveté on the part of some family members. I distinctly recall one impassioned mother of a man in prison for murder rebuking me for treating her son "like a criminal." I told her that was precisely what I was trying to do.

Criminal justice interest groups almost universally have the best of stated intentions. But whether they are Mothers Against Drunk Driving, Parents of Murdered Children, other victims' rights groups, or watchdog groups looking out for the interests of defendants or inmates, their advocacy can be very beneficial or, because of a lack of objectivity and attention to accuracy, can be destructive of the reputations of the people they target. To the extent such groups enter the legislative arena and pursue changes in the law they deem appropriate, I applaud their advocacy. I credit Mothers Against Drunk Driving for leading a campaign that succeeded in changing drunk driving laws in the United States from very lenient to very strict. When I started as a deputy district attorney in 1977, the average person convicted of drunk driving was given a $100 to $150 fine and no other consequence. Today, even if a defendant avoids jail time because it's a first offense, he'll pay a very high price for his indiscretion.

He'll lose his license for some period of time. He'll go to alcohol education and possibly treatment. By the time he pays his lawyer and all the fees and costs, he'll be out at least $3,000. And he'll also do community service. Repeat offenders are incarcerated for some period of time. As a consequence of such changes in the law, traffic deaths in Colorado due to alcohol were cut in half.

I saw similar progress by domestic violence advocacy and prevention groups who caused legislators, prosecutors, and judges to give proper focus to a very serious societal problem. When I started as a deputy district attorney in 1977, our office had a "drop charge day." Every Wednesday afternoon at 2:00 P.M., victims, almost always women and often evidencing fresh bruises or other visible injuries, would line up in the office reception area and fill out forms requesting the district attorney to drop charges, usually against a husband or boyfriend. It was a very depressing sight, and we knew we were doing nothing to address the underlying problem. By the time I was elected district attorney in 1988, largely because of the efforts of domestic violence advocacy groups, we were routinely refusing to drop charges simply because the victim requested it. We sometimes forced a victim to testify in order to secure consequences for the abuser, making sure he knew it was the state, not the victim, that was pressing the matter. We also provided much-needed counseling and access to other services, including a shelter for the victim and her children. Allowing women to escape from domestic violence situations has led to reduced levels of victimization. But over time, in some communities, I watched the pendulum swing too far. I supported police policies that mandated arrest and issuance of restraining orders upon probable cause that a crime had occurred, but it got to the point that some departments had an "arrest somebody" policy regardless of whether there was probable cause to arrest a particular individual. Even with good intentions, arrest without probable cause is unconstitutional.

I have also seen criminal justice interest groups, or individuals whose affiliation with them is well known, be driven by the passions of a particular case and, without sufficient information, make unwarranted allegations against judges or prosecutors who are unable as a matter of professional ethics to adequately respond.

Frankly, I don't propose a remedy for my concerns about criminal justice interest groups. An intelligent and informed media scrutinizing the claims of such groups is the ideal. The advocates have free speech rights and so does the media, regardless of how well informed or ill informed they may be. I simply suggest that while such interest groups have brought great reforms and improvements to the justice system, special interest politics is not always conducive to the effective administration of justice in a particular case.

Policing the Police

In some governmental structures, such as the former Soviet Union, the police and prosecution are virtually one and the same. The criminal investigative function and the prosecution function are done by the same agency under the same leadership. It may create some efficiencies, but it also creates some serious pitfalls, not the least of which is the lack of accountability that arises when the police don't serve as a watchdog over the prosecution and vice versa. In the United States, as any fan of the long-running TV show *Law & Order* is well aware, the investigative and prosecution functions are largely separate and distinct. Local police departments, sheriffs' offices, and state police investigate alleged crimes and refer the results to the appropriate prosecution agency. Federal agencies such as the FBI, the Drug Enforcement Agency (DEA), the Bureau of Alcohol, Tobacco, and Firearms (ATF), and others, refer the results of their investigations to the U.S. attorney. The prosecutor reviews the results of the investigation and determines whether the evidence is sufficient to warrant the filing of criminal charges or presentation of the case to a grand jury. In such a system, there is the very real potential for tension between the police and the prosecution. The prosecutor may be critical of the quality of the investigation undertaken by the police. The police may believe a case has been improperly declined for prosecution. While most such disagreements are professionally resolved and take place outside public purview, when they do become public they're often contentious and one side or both can suffer political consequences. Prosecutors, police chiefs, and sheriffs can lose their jobs when such tensions get out of control. Good prosecutors spend considerable time participating in the training and indoctrination of new law enforcement officers to ensure they understand the differing roles of the police and the prosecutor. And they work hard to cultivate effective working relationships with the detectives or agents who bring the cases. They are readily accessible to discuss the progress of cases and to advise what needs to be done to make a case prosecutable. An elected or appointed prosecutor needs to establish relationships with the heads of police agencies that are based on honesty and mutual trust. Each needs to believe the other will not undermine them to the public or media.

There are other areas of possible tension in the police-prosecutor relationship. The police should expose any perceived unethical conduct by the prosecutor in handling a case, and prosecutors are ethically obligated not to tolerate any lack of integrity by the police in the investigation of a case or the presentation of evidence to a court or grand jury. In any documents presented to the court to procure warrants, the prosecutor cannot knowingly tolerate misstatements or deceit by the officer signing the affidavit. As indicated earlier, I suspect, based on many years of experience, that one of the most frequent ethical lapses by prosecutors involves the failure to expose fudging of the truth by police agents. The temptations are obvious. The law of search and seizure and the law regarding suspect statements have become so complex that it's not unusual for the U.S. Supreme Court to split 5–4 as to whether the police acted properly. Yet, the officer on the street is expected to make a proper decision in a split second. The seeming unfairness of that reality may cause a police officer to conclude that tailoring the facts to avoid suppression of physical evidence or a confession is justified. But righteous prosecutors must never let the police believe such conduct is acceptable, even in cases in which the evidence of guilt is overwhelming. If they send the message loud and clear early in their career, the police will get the message. Individual prosecutors acquire reputations in the law enforcement community that follow them throughout their career.

Finally, in our justice system, the prosecutor is sometimes called upon to consider whether law enforcement agents themselves have violated the criminal law. It's a necessary and important part of the prosecutor's responsibility to the public. Unlawful use of force cases are especially difficult to handle in a manner that engenders public confidence. Fact finders, whether they are judges or juries, rightly give great deference to the police in their decisions about the use of force. Recognizing the difficulty and danger inherent in the job, they properly tend to give the benefit of the doubt to an officer. If there's a colorable claim that he acted to protect himself or others, they will not convict a law enforcement agent. Prosecutors should take this into account in analyzing use of force cases. But when it's clear the police beat an arrestee or shot someone in wholly unjustifiable circumstances, the prosecutor must take them to task. I prosecuted a few such cases, and, as an attorney in private practice who represented the Colorado Springs Police Protective Association, I defended several officers accused of excessive force. They are emotion-filled cases, but the proper investigation of them and the proper prosecution of them when warranted is absolutely essential to ensure public accountability for law enforcement.

Police dishonesty, when criminal in nature, must also be dealt with harshly and unequivocally. As district attorney, my office prosecuted a police officer who stole $3,000 in cash from a person he stopped for a traffic violation, confident the money was drug proceeds and the driver wouldn't report it missing. The cop was wrong. The driver reported it, and there was just enough corroboration from another officer to convict the wayward cop. But my most memorable prosecution of dishonest cops involved a scandal that rocked the Denver Police Department in 1990 and that I alluded to in the segment on special prosecutors. I was appointed special prosecutor to investigate two Denver police officers dubbed the "super cops." They were accused of paying certain informants to solicit criminal compatriots to commit burglaries and robberies. The paid informant would drive the coconspirators to the crime scene and then abandon them. The two corrupt cops, having been monitoring the event, would catch the crooks in the act and, because the media had been tipped off, often on camera. When defendants claimed they were set up, skeptical prosecutors, judges, and juries had little reason to believe them—until the number of defendants making the allegation in cases involving the same two cops was impossible to ignore. It was a very tough case to prosecute, because the paid informant witnesses were hard-core criminals with serious credibility problems. I was pleased to get convictions for official misconduct and to end the law enforcement career of the architect of the scheme. I found it very disconcerting that the officers' direct supervisor wrote a letter to the judge before sentencing lauding the wrongdoers for "doing what it takes to get bad guys off the street." He was obviously part of the problem. The end did not justify the means.

As Colorado attorney general, I'm chair of the state's Police Officer Standards and Training Board. That board revokes the peace officer certification of approximately two dozen officers each year for some sort of misconduct, usually the commission of a crime. It's important that the public recognizes that bad conduct by law enforcers is not tolerated.

Policing the police is a very difficult but very necessary part of a prosecutor's job.

Forensic Science

In the late 1980s, certain neighborhoods in Colorado Springs were terrorized by a serial rapist. Dozens of women were victimized. The perpetrator's modus operandi was such that his victims never saw his face and had little information to provide to the police to aid in their investigation. But in one incident, the rapist got sloppy and left behind a piece of physical evidence that caused the police to focus on a particular individual as a possible suspect. The police consulted with a deputy district attorney in my office and decided to utilize a recent forensic science breakthrough, DNA fingerprinting, in an attempt to solve the rape cases.

Deoxyribonucleic acid (DNA) is the chemical structure that forms chromosomes. A piece of a chromosome that dictates a particular human trait is a gene. DNA is two strands of genetic material spiraled around each other. The chemical structure of everyone's DNA is the same, but the sequence of what is called the base pairs of DNA is unique in each person. These unique sequences are the basis for DNA fingerprinting.

Several of the rape victims had gone to the hospital and had vaginal swabs taken to preserve the perpetrator's seminal fluid. The police secured a court order allowing them to take hair and fluid samples from the suspect for the purpose of comparing the DNA in the samples to that in the seminal fluids recovered from the victims. The FBI lab reported a DNA match between the samples taken from the suspect and the seminal fluid recovered from each of the victims. But Colorado courts had never previously ruled on the admissibility of DNA evidence. This would be the first case in which they did so. In *People v. Lindsey*, the district attorney's office succeeded in getting the evidence admitted at trial, and Gregory Lindsey was convicted of numerous counts of rape and sentenced to more than two hundred years in prison. On appeal, the Colorado Supreme Court for the first time recognized the validity of DNA fingerprinting and affirmed the convictions.

Shortly thereafter, the Colorado Springs Police Department began to review unsolved murder cases to determine if DNA testing could be of assistance in solving them. In one case in which the murder was committed more than fifteen years before, the police had identified a suspect with a motive to kill the victim, but they had no evidence that put the suspect at the scene of the crime. One of the pieces of evidence recovered at the crime scene was a cigarette butt. Fifteen years after the crime, the cigarette butt was analyzed and DNA was found in saliva still present on the butt. A saliva sample was secured from the suspect, and a DNA comparison with the cigarette butt revealed a match. The once stale case was prosecuted, and the defendant was convicted at trial.

The aforementioned examples demonstrate the remarkable capabilities that DNA fingerprinting has brought to forensic science. Each year thousands of cases are now solved that would not have been but for the development of this testing method. But DNA brought another equally important capability to crime investigation—the ability to exonerate a suspect. Since its recognition by the courts, DNA evidence has been used to overturn convictions in a number of cases, and many other suspects have not been charged because of the results of such testing.

Advances in forensic science, such as DNA fingerprinting, raise legal and ethical questions for law enforcement and prosecutors. Such forensic analysis can be expensive and time consuming, and it's not always conclusive. But if testable samples are available from a victim or a crime scene for comparison with a sample taken from a suspect, doesn't law enforcement have an ethical, if not legal, obligation to utilize available technology in an attempt to incriminate or exonerate the suspect? I would argue that it does. At a minimum, if samples are available for testing and they are not tested, the prosecution should be burdened to explain to the fact finder, whether a judge or a jury, the reasons why not, and the failure to do testing should be a consideration in determining whether a case has been proven beyond a reasonable doubt.

It has been my experience as a prosecutor that television and movies have created unrealistic expectations in the minds of jurors about the realities of forensic science. Such expectations became even more problematic when a TV series featuring forensic science became a top-rated show. Jurors seem to believe fingerprint evidence, blood evidence, hair evidence, or DNA evidence is available in every case. If it isn't, they question why it isn't, even if other evidence of guilt is overwhelming. Some legal commentators are calling it "the *CSI* effect." Good defense attorneys exploit this expectation. Good prosecutors work hard to overcome it.

I recall a bank robbery trial in which the teller identified the defendant in a lineup and in court. The defendant had been arrested the day after the robbery attempting to pass bills stolen in the robbery. A handwriting expert said the defendant's handwriting matched that on the demand note given to the teller. Imagine the prosecution's shock when, despite the evidence, the jury acquitted the defendant. Their explanation? The police hadn't found the defendant's fingerprints on the counter in front of the teller or on the demand note. They apparently discounted the testimony of a detective who indicated no latent prints capable of identification were recovered and that such circumstance was not unusual. One juror insisted she had learned on TV that fingerprints were always present. Jurors are developing similar expectations with regard to DNA. Prosecutors need to call experts to explain why such evidence was not recovered.

Forensic science will, no doubt, continue to make advances, some startling in nature, and these advances will greatly aid the capability of criminal investigators to solve cases by identifying the perpetrator. But to the extent that such scientific advances also provide a means of excluding or exonerating a suspect, they must be used by law enforcement for that purpose as well. The integrity of the criminal justice system requires it. The prosecutor's objective is not simply to convict, it is to do justice. And the prosecution should ensure that all the reliable tools available are utilized to secure justice.

The Media

Imagine a politician running for office and promising the electorate to withhold from the public most of the essential details upon which he bases the important decisions he's required to make as part of his job. It doesn't sound like a strategy designed for success in politics. Yet, public prosecutors, as elected officials and as lawyers licensed to practice law, face seemingly conflicting demands. On one hand, they're the representative of the public in the criminal justice system and obligated to zealously advocate for the public interest. On the other hand, they're ethically obligated not to comment on pending criminal cases, except to the limited extent permitted by professional canons of ethics. The possible sanctions for the violation of those canons include loss of a license to practice law. To my knowledge, no other elected public officials regularly operate under such constraints.

During the conduct of an investigation, prosecutors are ethically obligated to only publicly release such information as will aid the capture of the perpetrator or will prevent future crimes or adverse consequences from occurring. Once a suspect is arrested, the prosecutor cannot ethically comment on the evidence but must generally restrict his comments to the identity of the defendant, the charges and possible consequences the defendant faces, and the scheduling of court proceedings to follow. The Rules of Professional Conduct in every state bars a prosecutor from making comments about pending litigation that may have a substantial likelihood of materially prejudicing a defendant's right to a fair trial.

I can relate from personal experience that adherence to these ethical constraints, particularly in a very high-profile case where the press is ravenous for details and oblivious or unsympathetic to the prosecutor's obligations, takes an intelligent person of strong character and fortitude. It also takes a great deal of experience for a prosecutor to know exactly what can and cannot be said when the cameras are focused and the microphones are hot. By the time I was elected district attorney, I thought

I was pretty good at it. When I became U.S. attorney, the aggressiveness of the national press presented an even greater challenge. I once got a call from Connie Chung, who was with CNN at the time, at 6:00 A.M. on a cell phone no one but people in my office were supposed to know the number for. She assured me our conversation would be off the record. Luckily, I recalled she had told Newt Gingrich's mother the same thing, and I declined to talk with her. I was blessed to have an outstanding public information officer at the U.S. attorney's office that helped me negotiate through potential pitfalls.

But on both the state and federal level, I found the greatest challenge in ensuring compliance with ethical constraints didn't come from my own office, but from law enforcement agencies that conducted criminal investigations. The Professional Rules of Conduct in most states also impose a duty on prosecutors to make reasonable efforts to prevent those associated with the prosecution of a criminal case from making comments that the prosecutor is precluded from making. The competing interests that make such a task difficult are obvious. Law enforcement agents work hard to catch the bad guys. That's the essence of their job, and it takes place in relative obscurity. They, understandably, want credit when they succeed, and they'd like the public to know the details of the defendant's treachery and the details of their sometimes dramatic efforts to bring him to justice. And they may have no professional license to lose by revealing such details.

What constitutes "reasonable efforts" to prevent law enforcement agencies involved in a case from publicly revealing inappropriate information? I took two approaches. I would have personal discussions with law enforcement agency heads about the issue, and my public information officer would discuss the problem with his counterparts in those agencies. I would also send a letter at the beginning of each year to the head of each law enforcement agency we worked with, reminding them of our ethical obligations as prosecutors in regard to pretrial publicity and asking for their cooperation in meeting those obligations. We would set forth some basic guidelines to help achieve compliance, including having all postarrest public statements approved by our office. This strategy gave me some cover with the courts, if necessary, as well as a basis to take an agency to task for violating the guidelines we set forth. But, frankly, it was not uncommon for an agency to commit to compliance with the directive and then have someone in the agency leak information to the media, who, in turn, would promise to protect their source. We would then read or hear sensitive information in press coverage and have it attributed to "sources close to the investigation."

The key to a prosecutor's success in dealing with the media is absolute honesty, even when it's not reciprocated. It's vital to never lie to the media, but to let them know at the outset that your ability to be a source for them has significant limitations. Building a relationship of honesty and trust with those reporters your office works with every day is important and will pay off down the line. The media typically depends on a prosecutor's office for interesting stories and certain vital information and interviews. Any good public information officer will exploit that fact. The quid pro quo for cooperating with them in getting them the basic information they need is acknowledgment and acceptance of the prosecutor's constraints regarding pretrial publicity. The reality is that the media can get most of what they need from public documents filed in a case, including warrants and accompanying affidavits, complaints, informations, and indictments. It's entirely proper for the prosecutor's office to advise the media when and where such public documents are available.

I strongly caution fellow prosecutors not to provide off-the-record information to the media that could not ethically be provided on the record. A wise old newspaper reporter once explained to me that something told to a reporter on the record will be reported the next day, while something told off the record will be reported a week later, after a reporter has covered himself by being able to claim he has another source.

I found that the newspaper reporters who covered the courthouse on a consistent basis quickly learned the rules of the game. The good ones were aggressive but understood and respected the limits of the prosecutor's cooperation. The bad ones were sanctioned by complete noncooperation and tended to have short-lived courthouse beats. Television reporters were more problematic. Very few of them specialized in court coverage or took the time to learn the rules of engagement. It was much more difficult to build a relationship of trust. I found that prosecutors, generally, needed to be more wary with the electronic media, particularly investigative reporters. They were the least cognizant, and the least respectful, of ethical considerations.

The canons of ethics for lawyers in most states admonish them not to be unduly critical of judges. This admonition has the twofold purpose of preventing public confidence in the judicial system from being undermined and of recognizing the reality that judges are, for the most part, ethically unable to personally respond to criticism. But the obvious question of what criticism is due versus undue necessarily turns prosecutors into diplomats. As an elected prosecutor, I always felt it was part of my responsibility as the public's advocate in the criminal justice system to speak out and express disagreement when actions of the court seemed contrary to established law and contrary to the public interest. But, because of constraints on judges to explain their decisions or respond to criticism, I fully recognized the need for my comments to be professional and appropriately constrained. It was typical for me to begin by saying, "We respectfully disagree with the court's ruling," and briefly explain why. State judges may face periodic retention elections, in which case they may have a higher level of concern about what's said about them. In the case of life-tenured judges on the federal bench, respectful public expressions of discontent are the only remedy available.

Several years ago, a bar association ethics committee in Colorado issued an opinion saying it was improper for a prosecutor to inform a juror after a verdict, even in response to a question, that evidence in the case had been suppressed, or to publicly comment on the suppression of evidence as having possibly affected the outcome of a case. Such candor would "undermine public confidence in the criminal justice system," the opinion said. I vehemently disagreed. Are we suggesting the public is so stupid or unsophisticated that it can't handle the truth? Are we ashamed of how the system works? Are we concerned that there will be a groundswell of sentiment to change the system? I find hiding the truth about the operation of our justice system from the public abhorrent. The public needs further education about our Constitution and how it impacts the administration of justice. As long as posttrial comments about the suppression of evidence by either the defense or the prosecution are factual and not inflammatory, they should not be censored. The more the public knows about the workings of the system, the more likely they are to understand and accept it, or the more they will demand meaningful reforms.

We should cultivate understanding and respect for our justice system by educating our children about it and continuing to educate the general public about it whenever we have an opportunity. That requires effective and ethical use of the media and a recognition that many issues cannot be adequately dealt with in a thirty-second spot on TV. Prosecutors have a very important role to play in this educational process. The system should be transparent to the public except as necessary to protect the rights of the accused, the grand jury process, and matters affecting national security. The media is a means by which such transparency occurs. The presumption should always be in favor of open courtrooms. To the extent that ethical rules for lawyers are necessary to promote the effective administration of justice, good prosecutors will learn the rules and strictly adhere to them. They will play their role as advocate in a manner that promotes public understanding and respect for the law.

VI. The Federal Prosecutor

Today, virtually every matter that could be said to touch interstate commerce in even the remotest sense is vulnerable to federal jurisdiction and the federal criminal law.

After my service as an elected district attorney, I was convinced I would never again hold a public service job as interesting and as meaningful. That changed on July 30, 2001, the day I was nominated by President George W. Bush to be the U.S. attorney for the District of Colorado. I assumed the office on an interim basis on August 31, 2001, and was confirmed by the Senate forty-five days later. I served as U.S. attorney until January 1, 2005. In many respects, I found service as a federal prosecutor every bit as interesting and challenging as being a district attorney. In some ways, the jobs were very similar; in some ways, they were quite different.

The Constitution says nothing about who will exercise the prosecutorial power of the United States. So it was up to the first Congress to do so, and they did in the Judiciary Act of 1789. They created the position of U.S. attorney general, who would be the chief lawyer for the federal government. But given their penchant for decentralized power, they also provided that the president would appoint with the consent of the Senate "a person learned in the law" in each federal district to serve as U.S. attorney and represent the United States in all criminal and civil matters occurring within the district. George Washington appointed the first thirteen U.S. attorneys in 1789. Among them was a future chief justice of the U.S. Supreme Court,

John Marshall, who was appointed the first U.S. attorney for Virginia. Over time Congress has created ninety-three federal judicial districts in the states and federal territories. Many states now have multiple federal districts. The entire state of Colorado is a single federal district.

Many former federal prosecutors have spoken eloquently about what it means to represent the United States as a client. I recall reading an article in which Nicholas Katzenbach discussed his emotions as he stood before a racist southern judge during the height of civil rights unrest in the South in the 1960s. When the judge angrily demanded of him, "Just who is it that you speak for?" Katzenbach calmly replied, "Your Honor, I'm here to speak on behalf of the United States of America." Many of the applicants I interviewed for assistant U.S. attorney positions were leaving big law firm jobs paying much more money. When I questioned their motive, many of them explained that the opportunity to represent the United States was a long-term dream and the pinnacle of public service for lawyers.

Most of the former U.S. attorneys I've met indicate it was the best job they ever had, including a few that went on to high elective office. While I'll have to wait until the end of my career to attempt to choose, with the benefit of hindsight, the best job I had, there's no question the U.S. attorney's job is one that can have an enormous impact. I recall a comment my wife made the night my office had publicly confirmed it was investigating Qwest Communications for accounting fraud. The price of Qwest stock fell 50 percent, and the stock market as a whole fell several hundred points. "You never had that kind of impact on the stock market as a local district attorney," she said. And she was right. U.S. attorneys, as the prosecution arm of the United States, are frequently involved in litigation with national implications.

National and international events can make the U.S. attorney's job very interesting and challenging. My first day on the job as U.S. attorney was Tuesday, September 4, 2001. One week later, terrorists flew planes into the World Trade Center and the Pentagon, and the world was changed. On the afternoon of September 11, all ninety-three U.S. attorneys were on a conference call with U.S. Attorney General John Ashcroft. For the remaining term of the Bush administration, fighting terrorism would be the top priority of the Justice Department and, consequently, of the nation's U.S. attorneys. On November 29, 2001, the U.S. attorneys met with President Bush and Attorney General Ashcroft in Washington, DC, to discuss how the domestic war on terrorism would be waged. When the president shook my hand, he looked me straight in the eye and said, "You're on the front lines of this war; I need your help." Needless to say, I took his charge to heart. And fighting terrorism was fascinating work indeed. Suspected terrorist cells were monitored and uncovered. Numerous arrests were made, and more than five hundred people were deported. In the time I was U.S. attorney, about $150 million in terrorist assets were seized. Even in Colorado, there were classified investigations of suspected terrorists and a few prosecutions. As district attorney, I had felt the burden of fighting crime on behalf of the half a million residents of my judicial district. As U.S. attorney, I felt the burden of protecting more than 4.6 million residents of Colorado from terrorism.

U.S. attorneys' offices typically have greater resources than local prosecutors' offices. The salaries are typically higher, and the qualifications of applicants for assistant U.S. attorney positions are typically outstanding. During my tenure, we had thousands of résumés from attorneys who had graduated at the top of their class in the best law schools in the United States and who had excelled in private practice or in other government offices. It was not uncommon to receive applications from highly compensated partners in law firms who wanted to do something more meaningful. It was a tremendous pleasure to manage such high-caliber lawyers and watch them perform in significant cases.

While the caliber of assistant U.S. attorneys was very high, I believe Congress made a mistake in 1988 when it gave them a form of civil service protection. After that point, U.S. attorneys still had discretion as to who was appointed to supervisory positions, but it became very difficult to fire underperforming assistants. In the district attorney's and attorney general's offices I managed, lawyers served at the pleasure of their boss, and it was much easier to get rid of nonperformers. In public law offices, where the stress is high, the stakes are high, and the margin for error is small, the ability to quickly get rid of problematic lawyers is very important. As U.S. attorney, I had about seventy assistant U.S. attorneys. I viewed only three or four of them as underperformers. I figured I was lucky.

While U.S. attorneys have a certain amount of insulation from electoral politics that I found appealing, there's one aspect of life as a federal prosecutor that I found less desirable. The Department of Justice is a very large bureaucracy, and over time it's clear that more and more of the operations of U.S. attorneys' offices have been consumed by that bureaucracy. More and more of U.S. attorney discretion has become subject to the scrutiny of "Main Justice." By original design of Congress, U.S. attorneys are supposed to exercise a high degree of discretion independent of centralized federal power. But the Department of Justice is now routinely imposing various prosecution and crime-prevention initiatives on U.S. attorneys' offices that leave little room for the exercise of discretion. The Department of Justice frequently imposes the same prosecution priorities on every office without regard for dramatic differences in crime demographics. They evaluate the performance of U.S. attorney offices based on their adherence to Washington-imposed priorities and mandates, whether they're operating in Manhattan or rural Texas. In my view, the discretion afforded U.S. attorneys should include the determination of federal prosecution priorities in their district, and these priorities should be established in consultation with federal, state, and local law enforcement operating within the district. The Department of Justice can insist on priorities, such as terrorism, that are clearly national in scope, but others can be more localized depending upon the priorities of state and local authorities.

Former U.S. attorney general Robert H. Jackson alluded to the tension between national policy and local priorities when he spoke to the U.S. attorneys in April 1940:

> Your responsibility in your several districts for law enforcement and for its methods cannot be wholly surrendered to Washington, and ought not to be assumed by a centralized Department of Justice...
>
> At the same time we must proceed in all districts with that uniformity of policy which is necessary to the prestige of federal law.[*]

Most major cases, including death penalty cases, are now carefully scrutinized by Main Justice. During my tenure, several U.S. attorneys were instructed to ask for the death penalty in cases in which very experienced

---

[*] Jackson, Robert H. "The Federal Prosecutor," *Journal of the American Judicature Society* 24 (1940): 18, and *Journal of Criminal Law and Criminology* 31 (1940): 3–4; available at www.roberthjackson.org/Man /theman2-7-6-1.

attorneys in their offices had recommended against it. It was a common complaint among U.S. attorneys that Washington didn't trust them in such high-profile matters. In contrast, district attorneys and attorneys general in most states, including Colorado, have no supervisors and are ultimately only accountable to the people who elected them. They exercise immense discretion and establish and pursue their own priorities.

In the area of white-collar crime, much of the work done by federal prosecutors is different than that done by district attorneys. A great many of the federal criminal statutes are not derived from the Ten Commandments but, rather, from what I previously referred to as the fine print. That includes more esoteric sources of law like the Internal Revenue Code and the Code of Federal Regulations. These laws are much more technical and much less obviously criminal in nature than the bread-and-butter statutes that local prosecutors typically enforce. Bob Miller, a predecessor of mine as U.S. attorney for Colorado, summed up the difference this way: "The state prosecutor knows a crime has been committed and is trying to prove that the defendant committed it. Oftentimes, the federal prosecutor knows the defendant did something wrong and he's trying to prove it's a federal crime." That's a pretty accurate description, particularly in the case of complex federal white-collar cases.

Traditionally, U.S. attorneys are more selective about what cases they prosecute than are local and state prosecutors. Local prosecutors like to joke that U.S. attorneys only file cases that are "high-profile slam dunks." That's only partially true. There are other reasons that explain their selectivity in prosecution. The federal criminal code, unlike most state criminal codes, is not designed to promote plea bargaining and the efficient handling of a high volume of cases. While it's easy to plead a first-degree burglary down to second-degree burglary in state court, the federal system has far fewer lesser included offenses. While the definitions of culpable mental states, such as *intentionally*, *willfully*, *knowingly*, and *recklessly*, are typically uniform in a state criminal code, such definitions can vary from one federal crime to another. Further, and perhaps most significantly, U.S. attorneys have much less political proximity to constituents than do local prosecutors. Elected local prosecutors, elected sheriffs, and police chiefs who answer to elected city councils must be concerned about bad check cases, drunk driving cases, street corner drug deals, domestic violence, and other high-volume crimes that significantly impact the quality of life in a community. The FBI, the DEA, the Securities and Exchange Commission, and the Postal Inspection Service are federal law enforcement agencies with more-limited and more-defined roles, depending upon the mission given them by Congress. They have the luxury to establish enforcement priorities and, in cooperation with the U.S. attorney, to establish investigation thresholds and prosecution guidelines. Many of the cases federal prosecutors handle, particularly white-collar crime cases, tend to be larger and more complex than state prosecutions. But in recent years, U.S. attorneys have taken on some high-volume crime priorities, usually by direction of the Department of Justice. Federal firearms prosecutions and illegal immigration cases are recent examples.

In general, more goes into a federal prosecution than a state prosecution, and I'm not just talking about resources. I believe federal judges are more demanding of federal prosecutors than state judges are of state prosecutors, and I believe it's all a function of lower caseloads and the fact that no one holds federal judges accountable for how they treat litigants, including prosecutors. I can think of several instances in which federal judges required live testimony from witnesses on matters that prosecutors should be able to establish by documentary evidence under the Federal Rules of Evidence.

When you accept the president's nomination to be U.S. attorney, you know your tenure is tied to his and that your wonderful job will come to a relatively quick conclusion. So you're still subject to the vicissitudes of politics, although less so than in the case of direct election. I have yet to meet a former U.S. attorney who didn't think the job was well worth suffering the whims of presidential politics. As with any job, your ultimate goal as U.S. attorney is to leave the office better than you found it. You do that largely by the people you hire while you're there.

Federalization of Crime

For the first one hundred years of our nation's history, U.S. attorneys pursued a very limited number of federal crimes. Most federal criminal statutes were reflections of express constitutional provisions and included piracy, counterfeiting, treason, felonies on the high seas, thefts from the Bank of the United States, and arson of federal property. In contrast, over the last twenty-five years of our nation's history, Congress has added about twelve hundred new federal crimes. There are now more than four thousand federal crimes spread out through almost twenty-seven thousand pages of the U.S. Code and, through incorporation by reference, tens of thousands of pages of the Code of Federal Regulations. A task force of the American Bar Association set up to study the federalization of crime described the problem: "So large is the present body of federal criminal law that there is no conveniently accessible complete list of federal crimes."

Despite the explosive growth in federal crimes, 95 percent of all criminal prosecutions still take place on the state and local level. U.S. attorneys typically have dramatically smaller case loads than local prosecutors. As district attorney, my office of fifty prosecutors was responsible for handling forty thousand misdemeanors and four thousand felonies each year. As U.S. attorney, the criminal division of my office, also consisting of fifty attorneys, prosecuted a few thousand misdemeanor and petty offenses and six hundred felonies per year. And that's the way it should be. The Tenth Amendment dictates that the federal government exercise only the powers specifically delegated to it in the Constitution and that all other powers are reserved to the people or the states.

But over the last fifty years, Congress has tended to take a very broad view of the constitutionally delegated powers, and the courts have largely acquiesced in their aggressive approach. They have used the interstate commerce clause, for example, to expand federal jurisdiction over an incredible number of matters and have created a vast multitude of federal crimes in the process. Today, virtually every matter that could be said to touch interstate commerce in even the remotest sense is vulnerable to federal jurisdiction and the federal criminal law. So it's not surprising that critics of the increasing federalization of crime naturally point the finger at Congress and the federal courts, particularly the U.S. Supreme Court, as the culprits responsible for the federal power grab. I do too. But I'll never forget a conversation I had with Supreme Court Justice Antonin Scalia one afternoon on a Colorado trout stream. The subject was the expansion of federal power in general, and the federalization of crime in particular, and he convinced me that the public bears some blame for sanctioning the Seventeenth Amendment, which removed a principal check and balance the framers had created to prevent such a shift of power from occurring.

The Seventeenth Amendment, passed in 1913, provides for the popular election of U.S. senators. Prior to that time, by design of the framers of the Constitution, senators were elected by the states' legislatures. The framers reasoned that the separation and balance of powers, as well as the sovereignty of the states, would be best served if the people directly elected the U.S. House of Representatives, but that the Senate, the more deliberative of the two bodies, should be chosen by and accountable to the state legislatures. This would ensure that the federal government would not pass laws usurping state power or enact unfunded mandates. The U.S. senators understood such action would immediately lead to their removal from office by the state legislature. Not surprisingly, before 1913 there were virtually no unfunded mandates, and the power of the federal government was greatly restrained. And there were very few federal crimes.

In Federalist No. 46, James Madison dismissed as chimerical the fears that the federal government would usurp power from the states. He argued that the sympathy of Congress would lie with the states and prevent the federal government from enlarging its jurisdiction at the expense of the states. Madison obviously did not anticipate the passage of the Seventeenth Amendment.

Since the people began electing U.S. senators directly, the power of the federal government vis-à-vis the states has grown constantly and exponentially. Members of both houses of Congress want to be seen by their constituents as solving their problems. Solving a broad range of problems requires Congress to take a broad view of the interstate commerce clause and other delegated powers under the Constitution. Crime is one such chronic problem that Congress wants to appear responsive to. It seems in recent decades that Congress is always debating a crime bill. It's good politics. The result is that over the last several decades, Congress has created thousands of new crimes and has bragged to voters about it. Only legal scholars and other interested observers, including local prosecutors and state attorneys general, have voiced much concern about the trend. And only recently have federal courts shown any serious inclination to question the assertion of constitutional jurisdiction by Congress. In 1995 the U.S. Supreme Court revitalized the Tenth Amendment somewhat by striking down the federal Gun Free School Zone Act that made it a federal crime to possess a gun in a local school zone. The court found the matter fundamentally local in nature and unrelated to interstate commerce.

Having been a local, state, and federal prosecutor, I side with the critics of Congress that lament the increasing federalization of crime. As tempting as it is for Congress to pander to voters' concerns about localized crimes as diverse as domestic violence and carjacking, it should exercise constitutional restraint. There are plenty of crimes to investigate and prosecute that are unquestionably within the realm of delegated federal powers. Matters like terrorism, illegal immigration, securities fraud, and international drug trafficking can keep U.S. attorneys fully occupied. If Congress is incapable of exercising such restraint, the courts, citing the Constitution, should impose it upon them.

The Overcriminalization of U.S. Society

Closely related to the issue of federalization of crime is the claim of some that the criminal law has been transformed in the last four decades from being exclusively a sanction for serious morally culpable behavior to a sometime tool of do-gooders trying to accomplish a social or environmental agenda. At the root of the issue is the explosion of new federal crimes and the complexity of such crimes.

As indicated in an earlier chapter, the essence of criminal law is that certain acts are fundamentally contrary to the public welfare and need to be sanctioned.

The criminal laws enacted by the people reflect a moral consensus among them as to what behavior cannot be tolerated. While the public may not know all the details, like the difference in the mental culpability required for first-degree murder, as opposed to second-degree murder, they generally know the conduct is unlawful. If they kill, steal, or set things on fire, the law will take them to task. Knowledge that they're doing something wrong is at the essence of their criminal responsibility.

There's a growing group of critics who contend the criminal law, particularly the federal criminal law, has lost its moral bearings. They contend that too many new crimes not only do not require a culpable mental state but that the activity itself is not inherently wrong. The average person could commit the crime without any recognition they were doing something wrong, let alone subject to criminal sanction. One could collect a rock or a plant in a national park without knowing they were committing a crime in the process. A company could violate the highly complex import-export laws without knowing it. The controversy seems particularly acute in regard to the increase in federal crimes pertaining to the environment, workplace safety, administration of public assistance programs, health care privacy, and other areas of endeavor that were not traditionally a concern of the criminal law. Critics claim that mere negligent acts or failures to act in such areas of concern are now subject to criminal prosecution. Former U.S. Attorney General Ed Meese is among the most prominent of these critics.

I agree that the sanction of the criminal law should be reserved for morally culpable behavior. Except in the case of the most inconsequential petty offenses, offenders should have a general notion that what they're doing is wrong before they're subjected to criminal culpability for such behavior. And I agree that the federal criminal code presently outlaws some conduct that reasonably intelligent people wouldn't recognize as possibly criminal until authorities or their lawyer informed them they were in trouble. That's not right.

But I also believe some of the critics have overstated the problem, or at least the prevalence of prosecutions that manifest the problem. It's clear to me that prosecutors in their charging decisions and judges in their legal rulings have muted the concern somewhat by ensuring unsuspecting innocents are not prosecuted or convicted. I also know that it's commonplace, particularly in complex white-collar crimes, for defendants and their lawyers to tell juries and the public that they didn't know that what they were doing was wrong, when it's clear to investigators and prosecutors that they did. I've watched several corporate executives tell the public and juries that they didn't know enough about accounting standards to know they were doing anything wrong when they helped pad quarterly revenue to meet Wall Street projections and to earn big bonuses in the process. Even when they created reasonable doubt in the jury's mind, they didn't in mine. No one in their positions of responsibility could be that ignorant, and they wouldn't have gone to such lengths to hide their conduct if they weren't suffering a guilty conscience. That's why I was also unimpressed with much of the criticism of the U.S. attorney for the Southern District of New York for prosecuting Martha Stewart. The critics claimed Stewart should not be prosecuted for a cover-up when she was not prosecuted for the underlying crime of insider trading. But it was, in fact, her actions to frustrate the investigation that showed her recognition of wrongdoing. It was not innocent behavior. The jury agreed. I had similar feelings abut the prosecution of Scooter Libby, a White House aide to Vice President Dick Cheney. The fact that the initial crime being investigated, leaking classified information, was never charged does not mean that Libby should not be held accountable for lying to the FBI and the grand jury in the course of the investigation.

But I emphasize that my disagreement with those concerned about overcriminalization of U.S. society is one of degree only. The trend is a disturbing one, and prosecutors should speak out against it. People shouldn't have to rely on the good graces of prosecutors and judges to avoid criminal sanction for behavior that isn't morally culpable at its essence and not traditionally criminal in nature. The civil law can adequately deal with negligence and bad judgment and their consequences. To maintain the respect due to the social contract, the criminal law should be reserved for matters involving a culpable state of mind.

VII. The State Attorney General
Law Enforcer or Public Policy Maker?

When it comes to litigation, I still believe my only appropriate consideration should be whether the law has been violated and whether there's sufficient evidence to prove it in court.

When I was sworn in as attorney general of Colorado in January 2005, I understood my role would be significantly different than my work as a district attorney or U.S. attorney. Those public law offices did virtually nothing but litigation. The district attorney's office prosecuted criminal cases and had limited civil jurisdiction in consumer protection and public health areas. As U.S. attorney, my office did all the criminal and civil litigation for the United States in the District of Colorado. As attorney general, I understood I would be the legal advisor to all departments, agencies, and boards and commissions in the Colorado state government. My office would issue hundreds of legal opinions, both formal and informal, on a wide variety of subjects pertinent to the operation of the state. I also understood I would be involved in a broad range of civil litigation on behalf of Colorado, both as plaintiff and defendant, in addition to the criminal prosecution responsibilities.

But as to my role as the protector of the broad public interest, primarily in regard to Colorado's civil and criminal statutes relating to consumer protection and environmental protection, I still saw myself as assuming the familiar role of law enforcer. In fact, I would be the chief law enforcement officer in Colorado. I was the state's "top cop." It would be my job to enforce criminal and civil laws passed by the state legislature to protect consumers from fraud and deception. It would also be my job to enforce a variety of statutes enacted to protect the public from air and water pollution and other health hazards.

And I don't believe I was naïve. I was well aware that state attorneys general had been involved in some controversial litigation, including the massive civil suit against tobacco companies that had culminated in a settlement agreement in 1999 involving as much as $240 billion. I knew that many free market conservatives questioned whether that was a proper exercise of the state police power. I also knew that several attorneys general, like Eliot Spitzer in New York, had made quite a name for themselves taking on corporate America, and that many on Wall Street and elsewhere thought they were overreaching. No, I wasn't naïve, but neither was I fully prepared for what I found when I joined the ranks of state attorneys general.

In March 2005, I attended my first meeting of the National Association of Attorneys General (NAAG) in Washington, DC. In the weeks prior to the meeting, I was flooded with invitations to go to elegant private dinners and receptions hosted by large law firms or various corporate entities while I was in Washington. That's not something that occurred when I went to district attorney or U.S. attorney meetings. I was also invited to a meeting of the Republican Attorneys General Association (RAGA), which would take place the day before the NAAG meeting.

At the RAGA meeting, I met with other Republican attorneys general. Republicans held the job in twenty-one of the fifty states at the time. I had done a little research and learned that in 1998 there were as few as fourteen

Republicans. Out of concern for the alarming underrepresentation of Republicans, a few attorneys general and the Republican National Committee had founded RAGA. It was funded by individual and corporate contributors, many of whom were concerned about the growing activism among attorneys general that they believed was undermining free enterprise. RAGA had considerable success in the first couple of election cycles and was contributing significant funds to help elect Republican attorneys general. That led to the creation of DAGA, a Democrat counterpart, similarly dedicated to electing Democratic attorneys general. As time passed, many companies and interest groups contributed to both RAGA and DAGA. At a reception at my first RAGA meeting, I met dozens of representatives of various corporations and trade groups. I recall being a bit perplexed. What was the propriety and the necessity of such an effort to influence attorneys general?

When I came into the room for my first NAAG meeting, the scene looked very much like what I had experienced at National District Attorneys Association meetings and at meetings where all the U.S. attorneys got together. Tables were assembled to create a rectangle, and a name card and Colorado state flag marked the place where I was to sit. But when the NAAG president called the meeting to order, I noticed that, in addition to the attorneys general sitting around the table, there were more than a hundred people sitting at tables in the rear of the room. I whispered to a colleague sitting adjacent to me. "Who are all the people in the back?" I asked. He glanced at me in a way to suggest it was a dumb question and then smiled at me. "They're here to lobby you," he said.

And, indeed, they were. I've found that attorneys general are subject to intense lobbying in much the same fashion as legislators. But, instead of seeking your vote, the lobbyists are hoping that you will or will not sign on to an amicus curiae brief in the federal appellate courts, or, more importantly, that they can convince you to refrain from initiating or joining a lawsuit against their company or their interests. In some instances, an attorney general will be encouraged to join a litigation that is regarded as helping the lobbyists' company or industry. The lobbyists spend a great deal of time educating attorneys general about various issues that may become fodder for litigation in the future. And corporate America is now investing millions of dollars in attorney general races in the various states in an attempt to protect their interests.

How did it come to this? Fifteen years ago, no one cared much about state attorney general races. There was no RAGA and DAGA. NAAG meetings were quiet affairs largely free from outside pressures. A few of my attorney general colleagues who have held office for a long time lived through the transition and may have a better perspective than mine. But from what I've been able to ascertain and personally observe, the current situation is a confluence of interrelated trends. The bottom line is that attorneys general have become more litigious, more high-profile, and more politically ambitious. Precisely in which order these occurred or which trend led to others, I'm not certain. But the most logical analysis would seem to leave them in the order I described.

It's very clear that state attorneys general have become much more aggressive in pursuing what they believe to be the public interest and that consumer-protection litigation is the clearest manifestation of that fact. It also seems clear, in hindsight, that the tobacco litigation was a tipping point. Multistate actions involving numerous states against an offending company are now commonplace, and some attorneys general are not the least bit shy about taking on corporations or industries on rather novel legal theories. And only business-page editors, pro-business groups, and free enterprise think tanks seem to be very concerned. Former New York Attorney General Eliot Spitzer was incredibly aggressive, and, when he took on the New York Stock Exchange, a nongovernmental entity, for paying its CEO too much, only Wall Street insiders commented on the novelty of it. Bill Lockyer, the former attorney general of California, sued the world's major auto manufacturers in the last few months before he left office. He wanted California to recover damages for all the environmental damage caused by automobiles since their invention. It's California's contention that vehicles are a "public nuisance" the manufacturers have inflicted upon them. Not only is public nuisance a novel theory for a suit of this nature, but the case ignored the fact that the California legislature has imposed upon the auto manufacturers auto emission standards that are much stricter than the rest of the nation, and the companies have complied by specially manufacturing a significant portion of their fleets for sale in California. The suit also didn't acknowledge that it wasn't the auto manufacturers that built all the freeways on which the cars are driven. California's suit was summarily dismissed by a federal court, at which point the assistant attorney general in charge of it complained, "If there's a problem, there must be a remedy." Eliot Spitzer and seven other attorneys general also sued five of the nation's largest public utilities, seeking a reduction in carbon emissions, even though none of the utilities were located in their states. Current New York Attorney General Andrew Cuomo has taken steps to deter the construction of power plants in Kansas and Colorado. It seems state boundaries are no longer much of a deterrent to the reach of state attorneys general. Basic tenets of federalism are jeopardized by the notion that one state can control the actions of another.

In the last year some of my attorney general colleagues indicated they were contemplating bringing suit against social networking sites on the Internet. While I shared their concern about the threat to children from sexual predators who search out possible victims on these sites, and while I want the companies who own the sites to act responsibly by engaging in age verification or other steps that would protect children, I was curious as to a possible legal theory for a suit against the operator of a social networking site. "Attractive nuisance" was the reply. That's a legal theory that's applied when someone builds a swimming pool, or something else likely to attract small children, but refuses to put a fence around it, knowing full well that it might lead to injury or death for children. To my knowledge, the legal theory has not typically been applied in a way that requires people to anticipate the likelihood of a third party's criminal behavior.

Such an aggressive litigation posture by attorneys general has led critics to question whether they're engaged in a violation of the separation of powers. By using litigation to achieve public policy objectives they deem desirable, they are, in essence, legislating and regulating by litigation. They are shaping public policy, which is traditionally the legislative function. But the consent decrees by which they resolve the litigation and secure policy changes are not subject to either legislative or executive approval.

The aggressive litigation pursued by state attorneys general has caused them to assume a much higher public profile. Mainstream media has generally reported the attorney general activity favorably, and many attorneys general have assumed a populist image that plays well with voters. State attorneys general are now routinely running for higher office, including governor or U.S. senator. In fact, political insiders now often joke that AG means "almost governor" and NAAG is the "National

Association of Aspiring Governors." That, in turn, has, in my opinion, attracted more lawyers who have primarily a political background, rather than a legal background, to run for the office. It's very common now for successful state legislators to run for attorney general. They may or may not have extensive legal backgrounds in prosecution or in the private sector. Not surprisingly, in many of the meetings I've been in with fellow attorneys general that included discussions of actual or potential litigation or expressions of frustration about social or economic problems facing the country, some of my brethren sound a lot more like policy-making legislators than law-enforcing prosecutors. I've seen it in several contexts.

A Fortune 500 company based in Colorado was being threatened with a suit by attorneys general on the East and West coasts based on a very broad interpretation of their consumer-protection laws. Essentially, the attorneys general were suggesting the company, which was in the money transmittal business, had an affirmative duty to cross-examine its customers about their motive in transmitting money to foreign countries before doing business with them. In this way, they might deter their customers from participating in illegal foreign lotteries. Curiously, the attorneys general didn't think that government entities, including the U.S. Postal Service, doing similar transactions had such an obligation. After carefully researching the matter, I was certain no Colorado laws were being violated and questioned the basic legal theory behind the threatened litigation. At a meeting of several attorneys general and the CEO of the company involved, I asked the attorney general whose state was leading the charge, "Would you please explain to me the legal theory you're proceeding on?" He stared at me and said, "I'm insulted by that question." Apparently he was so insulted that he never bothered to answer it.

Despite the lack of a coherent legal theory by the accusers, the Colorado-based company chose to settle with the attorneys general before a suit was filed. They paid millions of dollars for a public education program for senior citizens that used money transmitters. The participating attorneys general bragged to their constituents about their good work. Why did the company settle? They settled because publicly held companies threatened with suit by state attorneys general can rarely afford to fight it out in court. I don't mean to suggest they can't financially afford to fight. They typically have sufficient profits and plenty of high-quality lawyers. But they also have an obligation to their shareholders to act in their best interests. And the fact is that, in most situations of this nature, a series of bad headlines in *The Wall Street Journal* or *The New York Times* about state attorneys general suing such and such corporation will have a more significant adverse impact on the market capitalization (i.e., stock price) of the company than any potential verdict five or ten years down the road. So the incentive to settle and avoid the bad headlines is very strong if the price to be paid isn't too large. The corporations know it, and the attorneys general know it. The cases typically settle.

This atmosphere has led to the attorneys general involving themselves in a broad range of societal problems. After Hurricane Katrina hit New Orleans in 2005, gas prices in the United States rose dramatically. The public was very angry, perceiving that the rise in prices was more a matter of corporate opportunism than the result of market forces. The attorneys general, always wanting to be perceived as diligent problem solvers, weighed in with their concerns. The Federal Trade Commission (FTC) and several attorneys general initiated investigations. I distinctly recall participating in a nationwide phone conference in which the FTC gave the attorneys general a preview of the report they were going to issue the next day. Essentially, the FTC investigation, as well as state attorney general investigations, found no systematic wrongdoing. They concluded the rise in prices was attributable to market forces, including the highly volatile spot and futures markets. Various attorneys general reported that, on the basis of their investigation, they saw no grounds for legal action. I thought that was the end of the matter and expected the phone conference to wrap up quickly. But a veteran attorney general from the Midwest made what I considered an amazing assertion. "Just because we've found nothing illegal doesn't make it right and doesn't mean we shouldn't do something about it," he said. "We need to do something about these obscene profits." I then, rather meekly, suggested that, absent a violation of the law, gas pricing wasn't our concern. It was up to legislative bodies to address taxation and policy matters. Only one other attorney general vocally expressed support for my suggestion. But it wasn't too long before market forces shifted. As the price of gasoline fell, public outrage and attorney general interest declined at the same rate. It was just one of many situations that led me to conclude my colleagues see themselves as much as policy makers as law enforcers.

Now, don't get me wrong. I believe it's wholly appropriate for me to weigh in on policy issues related to my statutory or constitutional jurisdiction as an attorney general. If the Colorado legislature, or Congress for that matter, is considering legislation related to the jurisdiction of my office, I routinely voice my opinion or even lobby the matter. My office also proposes legislation related to crime, consumer protection, and other matters that are relevant to the work of my office. But when it comes to litigation, I still believe my only appropriate consideration should be whether the law has been violated and whether there's sufficient evidence to prove it in court. I believe attorneys general should seek to solve problems only through remedies provided by the constitution and by the legislature. That can include common law remedies the legislature recognizes as within the attorney general's jurisdiction. I don't believe it's appropriate for attorneys general to pursue consumer protection or environmental protection litigation that doesn't derive from constitutional or statutory authority, but rather represents the attorney general's personal view of what constitutes the public interest. I suspect mine is currently a minority view. But it's clear to me that some of the litigation that state attorneys general are currently pursuing constitutes a circumvention of the legislative function in a manner that the governor or other executive officer could never accomplish. For example, if California's automobile emission standards are deemed insufficient to protect the public, isn't it up to the California legislature to act? Why should that decision lie with the California attorney general?

I respect and admire my fellow attorneys general. They are a well-motivated group, and I believe each is acting in a good faith belief that they are pursuing the public interest. But I respectfully disagree with many of them as to the proper role of the attorney general as a public policy maker.

The Wall Street Journal, the U.S. Chamber of Commerce, the American Enterprise Institute, the Competitive Enterprise Institute, and many other organizations interested in protecting free enterprise in the Unites States are leading the debate on the issue of activism of state attorneys general. I've heard several proposed solutions. One is to prohibit multistate actions by attorneys general. I don't personally see that as a remedy. State attorneys general have been involved in multistate actions since 1907 when they took on the Standard Oil Trust. Even if multiple states filed independent actions against a company or companies in federal court, it may well be determined, and correctly so, that consolidation of the actions in a single case is the most efficient way to handle the litigation. Further, my office has participated in numerous multistate actions against pharmaceutical companies, insurers, investment firms, and other defendants in which we concluded fraudulent or anticompetitive behavior by the defendant was clearly in violation of Colorado law, and the multi-state case presented a very efficient means of resolving our meritorious claims. We have, for example, caught pharmaceutical companies whose patents were expiring giving financial incentives to potential generic competitors to stay out of the market for a few extra years. That's a clear violation of the antitrust laws of every state.

I have also heard the suggestion that removing state attorneys general from the electoral process would reduce their litigious activism. I suspect that's true. Currently, the vast majority of state attorneys general are elected. Only a handful are appointed by the governor, the legislature, or the state supreme court. Appointment of all attorneys general, particularly by the governor, would reduce the likelihood of populist activism geared toward enhancing the political profile of the attorney general. If the attorney general was simply a cabinet member, as the position is in the federal system, he would be obligated to get the governor's acquiescence to commence high-profile litigation. That would certainly act as a filter of sorts. While I'd be personally inclined to support the appointment of attorneys general, the problem with the suggestion is that attorneys general in most states are constitutional officers who are second only to governors among state officials in influence and profile. The likelihood of the voters agreeing to amend the state constitution to eliminate the direct election of the attorney general is probably not high, particularly if adamantly opposed by a popular incumbent attorney general. The general public is largely oblivious to the issue of attorney general activism and is certainly not stirred to action by it.

I think groups interested in deterring attorney general activism are likely to achieve their greatest success by concentrating on curtailing some of the tools attorneys general have used to expand their influence. That will typically involve statutory changes. Legislatures can limit the powers given to the attorney general under state consumer protection laws. Some state consumer protection laws are dramatically broader in scope than others. And legislatures can limit the ability of the attorney general to transfer the police power of the state to private lawyers. Some of the most significant examples of regulation or policy making through litigation have come about when attorneys general hired private law firms to pursue litigation on a contingency fee basis. Colorado and other states have severely restricted the circumstances or the terms upon which that can be done. A good argument can be made that the state police power should only be exercised by a neutral public official who is not financially vested in the outcome, and that such neutrality is lost when cases are shopped to contingency fee lawyers.

I believe it's healthy that the issue of state attorney general activism is now a matter of considerable debate, albeit only in limited circles, and I would encourage the institutions and industries concerned about it to continue to foster the debate and to be politically involved in attorney general races that are impacted by the issue. They should also convey their concerns to state legislatures.

Because I still see myself as a law enforcer, I remain uncomfortable at the level of lobbying directed at attorneys general. But I have come to understand it as a sad reality of the current litigation climate. I'm a member of RAGA and a beneficiary of its political support. I distinctly recall an incident that pretty well sums up the practical realities of attorney general lobbying. Several months after I became attorney general of Colorado, I was visited by officials of a large beer company and a lobbyist for the company. They brought with them an attorney named Michael Moore, who used to be the attorney general of Mississippi. Moore is a very likeable guy and, by all accounts, was a very effective attorney general. In fact, it was Moore who began the now-infamous litigation against the tobacco companies when he hired a lawyer friend to pursue the case on a contingency fee basis. The lawyer and his firm are reputed to have made more than a billion dollars when the case was settled. Moore, now a highly compensated lawyer-lobbyist, had come to my office with the beer company officials to explain all the efforts the company was taking to deter underage drinking. The beer companies are concerned about attorney general scrutiny of liquor industry advertising and possible attempts to regulate it. As I walked out of the meeting, I jokingly whispered to an officer of the company, "Don't you think it's ironic that you hired Michael Moore to lobby for you." She wasn't amused. She looked at me in earnest and said, "We don't want to be the next tobacco." I understood completely.

VIII. Calls for Reform

Americans seem to have a love-hate relationship with their criminal justice system.

Throughout my legal career I have been fascinated by public attitudes about criminal justice in the United States. My conclusion, confirmed by polling that I've seen, is that the public has a rather pessimistic view of the system's ability to render justice in particular high-profile cases, but an optimistic view about the system's general ability to be fair. Americans seem to have a love-hate relationship with their criminal justice system. They don't hesitate to vigorously criticize it, but they appear confident that our system is the best in the world, and rarely do they suggest that another country has a better way of doing things. In fact, they don't take kindly to criticism of our system by other countries.

In November 2006, I traveled to Saudi Arabia at the request of the U.S. State Department. A Saudi citizen living in Colorado had been convicted in Colorado state court of enslaving his Indonesian maid and sexually assaulting her. He was sentenced to twenty-eight years in prison. His family was very well connected in Saudi Arabia, and they had used the Arab press to vilify the U.S. justice system as being biased against Muslims. The U.S. ambassador asked me to meet with Saudi leaders, including the King and Crown Prince, to correct the misinformation being spread about the case and to defend the prosecution of it. There was, of course, a huge cultural divide contributing to the problem. Under the Islamic law applied in Saudi Arabia, it took four eyewitnesses to convict someone of sexual assault. Needless to say, such convictions were rare. My trip got a significant amount of press coverage, and I was surprised how many people in Colorado, including the media, voiced outrage that our system of justice had been subject to foreign criticism. Not surprisingly, Americans who have traveled extensively seem most likely to be defensive of the U.S. judicial system.

But while Americans are defensive toward outside criticism, they are robust in their own. Judges are often accused of not being tough enough. Police and prosecutors are sometimes accused of being too zealous. Judges don't like sentencing guidelines or minimum mandatory sentences. Legislatures think such restraints are necessary to reign in liberal judges. Many Americans think juries in high-profile cases have been hopelessly inept as fact finders. Depending on your ideology, there are too many or too few people in prison. Many academics and editorial writers rail about the system being too harsh on drug offenders. There's also concern among many about the growing number of mentally ill defendants being incarcerated.

Some of the criticism of U.S. criminal justice runs headlong into the Bill of Rights and won't be rectified unless courts depart from longstanding constitutional interpretations or unless public dissatisfaction grows to the point that a constitutional amendment is possible. Neither scenario is likely. So defendants facing possible incarceration will continue to have a constitutional right to a jury trial. And courts are unlikely to abandon the exclusionary rule as a remedy for willful violations of the Fourth Amendment protection against unreasonable searches and seizures. State and federal legislatures will continue to determine what conduct is criminal and what range of penalties judges may impose for such crimes. But discussion of possible criminal justice reforms is healthy and should be encouraged. Based on the types of issues I've been asked to speak about through the years, it's apparent that certain areas of possible reform attract more attention than others.

Our trial system is the focus of a great deal of critical scrutiny. More experts are questioning the supposed supremacy of the U.S. justice system, and they're making articulate, forceful, and persuasive arguments. A law professor friend of mine, Bill Pizzi, wrote a book entitled *Trials without Truth* in which he suggests a series of reforms, many based on the operation of western European trial systems, that would make our trial system less burdened by procedural complexities and more capable of arriving at the truth. Any serious student of our system needs to pay close attention to such constructive criticism. And so much of the concern is centered on the perceived decline in the ability of juries to engage in reliable fact finding and to render just verdicts.

Jury Reform

While defendants will continue to have the constitutional right to have a jury determine whether the government has proven the charges against them, I have, over time, reached some conclusions about the subject of possible jury reform. In his book *The Jury*, Stephen J. Adler quite eloquently describes the issue of jury reform in the United States:

> The American jury system confronts us with a powerful contradiction: We love the idea of the jury, but hate the way it often works…We [have] an idyllic image of the jury. In the Salem witch trials, juries that embraced the madness ultimately called a halt to it. In the age of slavery, stubborn northerners helped to defang the fugitive slave laws by acquitting people who harbored runaways. In the movie *Twelve Angry Men*, one good man held out against a quick,

careless verdict and guided eleven others through debate and catharsis and onward to truth and justice. What's not to like about such a system?...But [in my research], I repeatedly encountered scenes that bore no resemblance to the high minded debate of *Twelve Angry Men*. Instead there were lots of sincere, well-intentioned people who—for a variety of reasons—were missing key points, focusing on irrelevant issues, succumbing to barely recognized prejudices, failing to see through the cheapest appeals to sympathy or hate, and generally botching the job...There is no question but that the jury system remains an enticing concept. It is the most potent tool for democratic self rule ever invented...The notion that the people who are making these most difficult decisions should come from the community and then return to the community that has to live with their decision is a satisfying prospect for a nation that takes democracy seriously. Our American heritage, with its emphasis on the rights of the individual, gives us compelling reason to preserve the jury system, even after the rest of the world has abandoned it, and to reform it as necessary to make it work more effectively.[*]

At the outset of a debate about jury reform, a fundamental question must be addressed: Is questionable and inaccurate fact finding an inevitable consequence of our jury system? I believe the answer is yes, but not to the extent that it often occurs. Given the nature of our jury system, it's inherently unpredictable, and, as illustrated earlier in this book's discussion of famous trials, questionable verdicts are nothing new. Even frontier justice was unreliable. In one Colorado mining town in the 1890s, a bank robber caught red-handed was quickly

---

[*] Stephen J. Adler, *The Jury: Trial and Error in the American Courtroom* (Times Books, 1994), xiii.

acquitted by a jury. The fact that he was allowed to sit through the trial, which took place in a saloon, with a loaded six-shooter in his lap, may have had some influence on the jury. But while I know from firsthand experience just how unpredictable juries can be, I join many others in a belief that our jury system could be improved to the point where it engenders greater public confidence. Some very basic reforms could make our juries perform more reliably and effectively.

Reform should begin with our current methods of selecting jury panels. The problem is not who is summoned to jury service. Random computer selection assures that a good cross section of the community is initially summoned to jury service. But the community profile then quickly begins to break down. According to Adler's research, only 45 percent of those summoned for jury service actually make it to the courthouse, and those excused beforehand are disproportionately the better educated and the ones most accustomed to a fact-finding process and to making tough decisions. It's not an elitist proposition to suggest this is problematic. Jury service should be for everybody (at least everybody who is literate, language proficient, and perhaps nonfelonious). But *everybody* includes successful people who find it an inconvenience to their other responsibilities. Jury service is a civic responsibility of the highest order, and we cannot allow citizens to manipulate their way out of it. We should excuse virtually no one from answering a jury summons. In return, we must make jury service as agreeable as possible. Every state should have a "one day or one jury" system; i.e., if you don't get selected to sit on a jury the first day you report, you're excused until you're randomly selected the next time. If you sit on a jury, you're excused when the case is completed. So no one has to sit around for a week or two without being on a jury. Jurors should have adequate notice and be expected to plan accordingly. Pay for jury service should be adequate to avoid severe hardship for the self-employed with modest incomes. Day care should be provided. Sequestration of jurors should be virtually abolished and judges should be accountable to move cases along in a manner that respects the service of jurors. All legal issues that can properly be decided before a jury is impaneled, should be.

How about sprinkling our jury panels with professional jurors who are paid to serve for an extended period of time and bring experience and greater knowledge of the law to the process? Does the Constitution prohibit such jurors with expertise? Mixed jury panels are utilized effectively in some European countries. It's worth discussing as a means of improving the fact finding capability of the jury.

How we conduct jury selection at the courthouse is also frequently a problem. It is increasingly common in high-profile cases to exclude from jury service anyone who knows about a case from reading a daily newspaper or watching news on TV, even if no actual bias or predisposition is shown. A dramatic example of that was the O. J. Simpson murder trial. Of the final twelve jurors, none said they read a daily newspaper or weekly news magazine. A few read tabloids. In such cases, the least informed survive the jury selection process and the most qualified decision makers do not. Exclusion from the jury by the court should be limited to showings of bias or predisposition and not be based simply on a showing that the prospective juror had knowledge of current events.

We should also seriously consider the whole issue of peremptory challenges—those challenges that lawyers can exercise against a juror without stating a cause. As a trial lawyer, I favored preemptory challenges because, as a colleague once put it, jury selection is a game of "Where's

Weirdo?" (as opposed to *Where's Waldo?*) in which you're trying to identify the strange person who might obstruct a desirable verdict, and once you find that person, you need to get rid of him, regardless of whether he acknowledges bias or prejudice that would lead to a challenge for cause. My problem is that U.S. Supreme Court decisions that have the effect of preventing the exercise of preemptory challenges against racial or ethnic minorities, or based on the sex of the juror, have so watered down the process that eliminating peremptory challenges and perhaps expanding the criteria for challenges for cause may result in making juries more representative of the community. As it is, while some members of the jury are essentially protected from peremptory challenge, one side or the other can use their challenges to effectively eliminate any managers or sophisticated decision makers from the jury.

We should also do a better job of instructing our juries about the task before them. In most states, juries are only instructed about the details of the law applicable to the case at the conclusion of the evidence, and then only in legalese. They should be given explanatory instructions before the evidence is presented so they will have a sense of what issues are important and what evidence may be relevant to resolve the issues. Letting jurors ask questions that are screened by the judge may well enhance their understanding of the evidence and appreciation of their role as fact finder.

Next—and this is a matter of considerable importance—our appellate courts must allow trial judges to take control of their courtrooms and protect juries from junk science and from irrelevant tangents and blatant appeals to sympathy. In one case my district attorney's office handled in which two seventeen-year-old boys went into the bedroom of the parents of one of them and shot them while they were sleeping, the jury received a self-defense instruction on the basis that the child of the victims was in imminent fear his parents might kill him, despite no evidence whatsoever that he was physically abused. That's just plain wrong. The jury told us afterward that allowing the instruction was very confusing to them because it seemed to give credence to a proposition that otherwise seemed ridiculous on its face. While it didn't work in that case, the same theory did lead to a hung jury in the first trial of Eric and Lyle Menendez in California, in which two sons, who didn't live at home, surprised and killed their wealthy parents, hoping to accelerate their inheritance. An expert witness was allowed to testify, in lieu of testimony from the defendants, that they felt abused by the parents and were acting in self-defense. Our local jury heard from the same expert that was used in the Menendez case. It seems he made a living testifying for the defense in "abuse-excuse" cases. Given the state of our society and the everybody-is-a-victim mentality that pervades it, our juries are, unfortunately, susceptible to such defenses. But we shouldn't compound the problem by allowing jury instructions that clearly don't fit the law and circumstances of the case. Appellate courts must support and not undermine trial judges who curtail the presentation of bizarre defenses that have no legal foundation. Incidentally, this proposition is supported by no less of a criminal defense advocate than Harvard law professor Alan Dershowitz in his book *The Abuse Excuse*.

Keeping junk science out of the courtroom is also essential to a reliable fact-finding process. While the prosecution must meet case law requirements showing the legitimacy of forensic evidence, judges fearing reversal are sometimes less inclined to exclude very questionable expert testimony on behalf of defendants. Unfortunately, creative counsel can find an "expert" somewhere to testify to virtually any proposition the defense might need. In

Trials without Truth, William Pizzi argues that a strong trial system requires that the trial judge be given more authority to determine what evidence is presented to a jury and appellate judges be given less authority to second guess their decisions. He is clearly right.

I have also come to the somewhat reluctant conclusion that the requirement of unanimous verdicts should be abandoned in the United States. The states that require a 10–2 vote for conviction cannot seriously be viewed as less protective of defendants' rights than those requiring unanimous verdicts. There has been an increase in hung juries over the last few decades attributable primarily to the phenomenon of unreachable jurors holding out against overwhelming evidence of guilt. Such cases are a significant waste of judicial resources. The cases infuriate the jurors who have reached consensus and dramatically undermine public confidence in the jury system.

These are only a few of the possible reforms that could make our jury system more effective and reliable. We should carefully consider all suggested reforms, but we should also accept the reality that unpredictable jury verdicts are with us to stay. Our jury panels reflect the moral ambivalence of our society. And in the debate about what to do about it, we should never lose sight of why our founding fathers insisted on a jury system. They did so to protect the individual from the state. On that score, the system remains very viable. We should pursue reforms that preserve the jury's integrity as a vehicle to protect the individual vis-à-vis the government, but that, at the same time, enhance public confidence in the ability of juries to do justice.

Reform of Drug Laws

Drug abuse is a problem as old as civilization itself. But criminalization of drug abuse is a relatively modern phenomenon. In the United States, various drugs have been illegal for about a century. But serious criticism of such laws seems to have its genesis in the 1960s and 1970s when large numbers of Americans became involved in illicit drug use and began to suffer the legal consequences of such involvement. Annual drug use surveys conducted by the Office of National Drug Control Policy (ONDCP) show that the percentage of Americans using illicit drugs rose steadily until it peaked at 14.1 percent in 1979. The response was harsher penalties enacted by Congress and state legislatures to deter the growing problem. As prison populations grew and the cost of incarceration soared, so did the chorus of criticism, particularly from academics, editorialists, and the criminal defense bar. By the 1990s, the debate was raging, despite the fact that the level of illicit drug use had dropped sharply to 5.8 percent of the population by 1992.

I've been closely involved with the criminal justice system as a prosecutor, prison administrator, and director of a community corrections board over a period spanning almost thirty years. I've carefully listened to the debate about decriminalization of drugs and about punishment versus treatment. I've contrasted the assertions of the critics to the reality I witnessed in my various roles. Just as I have as to many other aspects of crime and punishment, I've reached some conclusions about the myths and realities of drug laws.

It's been my observation that arguments in favor of legalization of drugs are much more popular in academia, think tanks, and on editorial pages than they are among law enforcement and drug treatment professionals who must deal with the ravages of drug abuse every day. I've also found very few recovered drug addicts who support legalization. And, finally, I've found that the members of the public who live in or near drug-ravaged neighborhoods are the most vociferous in demanding law enforcement intervention.

Most of the credible arguments in favor of decriminalization are rooted in economic theory. If drugs weren't illegal, they could be obtained more cheaply (although it's unclear whether that would be under government auspices or from pharmaceutical companies). Violence and other adverse impacts of the current lucrative drug trade would be drastically reduced. Drug users would not have to burglarize our homes to afford their drug habit. Because we wouldn't be spending so many dollars on law enforcement, there would be more money to spend on drug education and rehabilitation. Or so the argument goes.

My problem is that no advocate of decriminalization can say with any degree of confidence, or on the basis of any experience, that legalizing presently illicit drugs would result in less human destruction and fewer people ruining their lives and the lives of people around them. In fact, there's every reason to believe legalization would increase human tragedy. Legalizing drugs would let the price of drugs fall to its competitive rate plus, presumably, taxes and marketing costs. Most knowledgeable analysts suggest the resulting market cost would be one-third to one-fifth of the black market price. But something else would fall more dramatically—the risk cost. Most of the non-health-related hazards associated with buying drugs, like getting arrested, would be eliminated. That reality might be more important than the lower purchase price in determining the consumption rate of drugs. Virtually everyone who has carefully analyzed drug use believes that a legal regime would lead to greater consumption. But how can we be sure? There's more than common sense to convince us. The fact of the matter is that legalization of drugs has had that result in England, the Netherlands, Switzerland, and other countries where it has been tried.

A significant percentage of the new users that would result from legalization would become an economic burden on society. They would be unable to keep a steady job. Unless they're adequately supported by welfare payments, crime becomes a logical source of needed income. Even if the legal drugs were cheaper, addicts would need a social subsidy or the proceeds of crime to support their lifestyle, however meager it might be. So even if the manufacture, sale, and use of drugs was no longer a crime, the total number of drug-related crimes would likely increase. Further, a high percentage of all crime, including violent crime, is committed by persons directly under the influence of drugs. Legalization would exacerbate that problem, not reduce it. There would be more experimenters, eventually more addicts, and more crime. So, one of the foremost arguments of legalization proponents, that it would reduce crime, is fallacious. Add to the list of resulting harms more deaths from overdose, more drug-affected babies born to addicted mothers, more accidents caused by drug influenced drivers, and fewer people able to safely perform at work or act as competent parents or guardians.

Many decriminalization advocates seem convinced that virtually no one refrains from engaging in conduct because it's unlawful. They say the war on drugs is a failure because so many people still use illicit drugs. But curiously, they don't say that about the war on homicide, the war on burglary, or the war on auto theft. In essence they're convinced the drug problem couldn't be any worse, so legalization could do no harm. Research shows the opposite. The drug problem could be, and has been, much worse. The vast majority of Americans don't use illicit drugs, and we have made considerable progress in significantly reducing the percentage that do. As indicated previously, the ONDCP Household Survey shows the portion of the population using illicit drugs has been cut in half over the last twenty-five years. Seventy percent of high school seniors have never used an illicit drug. And it's important to consider why they haven't. Two studies in New Jersey and California, in which high school students who didn't use drugs were asked why they didn't, showed the number-one reason was the fact that drugs were illegal. The number-two reason was potential harm to their health. A large segment of Americans refrain from engaging in conduct because it's illegal and they fear the consequences. That explains the significant decline in drunk-driving deaths that resulted from increased penalties. Designated drivers are a phenomenon produced by fear of the law. And it's such deterrence that caused the decline in rates of illicit drug use since the peak in the late 1970s.

Other advocates of decriminalization cite the hypocrisy in having alcohol legal and other drugs illegal when the consequences of alcohol use in our society is so devastating. I've never viewed that argument as supporting the legalization of presently illicit drugs. No one can seriously suggest that the legalization of alcohol has lessened the human tragedy caused by abuse of the drug. Discussions about the failure of prohibition omit the fact prohibition reduced the national consumption of alcohol by at least 50 percent. Prohibition failed because the widespread use of alcohol among all segments of the population led to a lack of support by the American people for the effort. Prohibition of presently illicit drugs, on the other hand, has the support of an overwhelming percentage of Americans. That's why legalization proponents have fared poorly in getting legislatures or voters to change drug laws and have resorted to deceptive schemes like medicinal marijuana to get the nose of the camel under the tent. Straightforward legalization efforts have failed miserably. Finally, the fact is that alcohol is a different kind of drug than most illicit drugs. While alcohol is a dangerous drug, it can be ingested in subintoxicating doses, and not everyone drinks alcohol for the purpose of getting drunk. In contrast, the reason people take illicit drugs is to become intoxicated by them. Many illicit drugs have very different addictive qualities and capabilities than alcohol.

Many argue that drug treatment and law enforcement are incompatible approaches to the drug problem. Drug abuse is a health problem, they argue, and should not be a criminal justice concern. They are naïve, and they are wrong. Drug abuse needs to remain a criminal justice issue in order to be effectively addressed as a health issue. The reality is that the criminal justice system is far and away the principal means by which drug affected people are referred to education, therapy, and treatment programs. Specialized drug courts have been particularly effective in this regard. Approximately 90 percent of people in alcohol and drug treatment are there under court order. Without law enforcement intervention, most drug treatment programs would be in search of clients. Most drug treatment professionals acknowledge that drug addicts rarely volunteer for treatment, and rarely do they remain in treatment, absent some compulsion to do so. Legalization means a loss of coercion, and that means more addicts and fewer of them being treated for their addiction. Incidentally, studies indicate the success rate of those coerced into drug treatment is the same as those who volunteer for it.

Much of the opposition to drug laws is driven by a tremendous myth about who's in prison for drug offenses. First-time offenders under the possession and use laws of Colorado and most other states are not shuttled off to prison. They're placed in diversion or on probation and ordered into education and treatment programs. Only when they continually reoffend or commit other serious crimes are they sentenced to prison. As indicated in another chapter, my analysis of the Colorado prison population when I was executive director showed that only a quarter of the inmates had never been involved in a violent offense, and that this group of truly nonviolent offenders averaged almost three prior felony convictions apiece. Drug abusers only go to prison when they fail at all the available alternatives or commit serious property or violent crimes. To the extent that is not true in other state systems or in the federal system, we should consider changes in the law.

In my opinion, there are simply no valid compelling arguments to suggest legalization of presently illicit drugs is an appropriate moral or societal solution to the drug problem in the United States. We need to reduce the demand for drugs, and you don't do that by waiving a surrender flag and sending a mixed message to our children. Capitulating to a problem is not a solution to the problem. We can and should argue about what sorts of penalties are necessary to accomplish deterrence, and we should search for creative and effective ways to deal with substance abusers in the criminal justice system, but we must retain a deterrent. A persistent level of law enforcement, combined with ever-increasing educational and treatment efforts to reduce demand, provides the best opportunity for success. The strategy has worked to reduce levels of drug use in the United States over the last thirty years. I see no reason to give up the fight.

Mental Illness in the Criminal Justice System

As a young prosecutor, I tried a case in which the defendant, a male in his mid-twenties, was charged with criminal trespass. He had broken into a museum during the night and was found sleeping on the floor the next morning. He was a repeat offender. He was also, in my opinion, criminally insane. In Colorado, as in most states, the McNaghten rule for insanity applied. Under the McNaghten rule, a defendant is insane if, by reason of mental disease or defect, he is unable to distinguish right from wrong or unable to adhere to the right. It's a difficult test to meet. But this defendant, a diagnosed schizophrenic, clearly met it. Yet, his very competent public defender didn't let him plead not guilty by reason of insanity. If he had, I would have stipulated to it. Rather, his attorney simply asked the jury to acquit him because he was "nuts." He didn't plead not guilty by reason of insanity because a defendant found insane in Colorado is hospitalized indefinitely in a mental institution until he meets the burden of showing he's no longer a danger to himself or others. Because of the nature of his crime, the trespasser faced a sentence of one year in prison. His attorney felt that was a better alternative than an indefinite commitment to a mental hospital.

On the other hand, I have been involved in at least two murder cases in which defendants who had graduated from college, who had engaged in extensive premeditation before the crime, and whose motive for committing it was fairly apparent, pled not guilty by reason of insanity. I suspect their hope was the jury would conclude no one with brains would do something so stupid unless they were insane. A plea of insanity was worth the risk because long-term hospitalization was more attractive than a life sentence in prison.

The risk-and-reward analysis described above leads to an irony. Of the dozen or so defendants I prosecuted in my career that I believed to be insane under the McNaghten rule, only one was charged with murder (an arson that killed a transient). The others were charged with relatively minor crimes, and none of them pled not guilty by reason of insanity. The result of this irony is that relatively few defendants are found not guilty by reason of insanity and those who are have typically committed very serious crimes. In one case I recall in Colorado Springs, a paranoid schizophrenic had walked out of his mother's house, where he lived, into a neighbor's house across the street and gouged out the eyes of a babysitter he'd never met before. He was found insane and remained in a mental institution until his death.

But even the most bizarre behavior does not typically involve insanity. In one of the most publicized cases I was ever involved with, a twenty-two year-old male posed as an eighteen-year-old female and enrolled in high school. The imposter became captain of the all-female cheerleading team and even dated the quarterback of the football team. While the young man obviously had mental health issues, insanity wasn't one of them.

There are a few apparent malingerers in our mental hospitals who successfully pulled one over on a prosecutor, judge, or jury seeking a rational explanation for a heinous crime. One of my first murder trials involved an Air Force captain named Ron Ball. Ball was the top assistant to the four-star general in charge of the North American Air Defense Command (NORAD). He was clearly considered by the Air Force to be general officer material. Ball had a girlfriend who was madly in love with him. They had met at the Pentagon, where she was a secretary, and she had followed him to his assignment at NORAD in Colorado Springs. After dating for three years, the girlfriend wanted to get married. Ball kept putting her off. Eventually, the girlfriend started dating another guy. That got Ball's attention. He tried unsuccessfully to get her back. Then one day he parked his car in the parking lot across from the ex-girlfriend's apartment and waited. He was in his Air Force uniform. When the new boyfriend came to pick her up, Ball encountered them both as they got into the boyfriend's pickup truck. Ball calmly asked the new boyfriend to get out of the truck so they could "talk about things." The boyfriend said there was nothing to talk about. After Ball asked again and was refused again, he pulled out a Vietnam service revolver and shot the boyfriend point-blank in the head. He fell over on the screaming girlfriend's lap. Captain Ball calmly walked away, got in his car, and drove off.

When he was arrested several hours later in the washroom of a Mexican restaurant, Ball claimed to have no knowledge of the crime and vehemently denied committing it. The murder weapon was never found. But Ball's high-priced defense attorney had some evidentiary problems. The girlfriend was a good witness, two ladies had observed Ball "lying in wait" across the street, and there was microscopic blood splatter on his Air Force uniform. The solution? Allegedly over Captain Ball's objection, his attorney pled him not guilty by reason of insanity. He hired two high-priced psychiatrists who diagnosed him as having suffered from a form of temporary insanity called hysterical neurosis, dissociative type. They claimed that a highly rigid individual, when confronted with emotional trauma, can snap and go into a fugue state in which he can do something that appears highly deliberate but over which he has no control, and subsequently has no memory of having done. Their testimony, in combination with a handsome and intelligent Ball crying on the witness stand and lamenting, "I didn't do it, I didn't do it!" had more of an impact on the jury than the low-priced state hospital doctors who said Ball was simply a jealous lover. A jury of nine women and three men found Ball not guilty by reason of insanity. Not surprisingly, the captain made a very rapid recovery from his mental illness and only two years later he was able to convince another jury that he was no longer a danger to himself or others. He was released from the state hospital and, last time I heard, was working as a dance instructor. He also collects a disability pension from the Air Force.

Approximately six months after Ron Ball was found insane, at a meeting of the American Psychiatric Association, the delegates voted to remove hysterical neurosis, dissociative type from the diagnostic manual for mental illness. Apparently, it had been approved as a diagnosis on a very close vote a few years earlier and was subsequently rejected on a similarly close vote. I've never failed to point out to juries in subsequent cases when the diagnostic manual was being used by the defense that psychiatric diagnoses make their way in and out of manuals by a vote of designated members of the psychiatric profession.

I believe, based on my experience with the insanity defense and other mental health–related defenses, that the purpose of psychiatry, to explain human behavior, and the purpose of the criminal law, to hold people accountable for their antisocial behavior, have never been satisfactorily melded in the criminal justice system. Yet, we continue to try to do so, with often inconsistent results.

In my mind, issues about the insanity defense are only a small part of the mental health issues confronting the criminal justice system. By the time I became director of the Colorado correctional system in 1999, almost 20 percent of the eighteen thousand inmates in the system had been diagnosed as mentally ill when they came into the system. Only a tiny fraction of them met the definition of insanity. The rest were just mentally ill, and they had generally committed very serious crimes such as murder, assault, robbery, and sexual assault, including sexual assault on a child. When I began to look for an explanation for the presence of so many mentally ill people in prison, it didn't take long to find it. In 1965 there were six hundred thousand people in mental health institutions in the United States. By 2000, despite the fact that the population had almost doubled, there were only sixty thousand. In Colorado we had gone from six thousand institutionalized patients in 1965 to about seven hundred in 2000. In the 1970s and 1980s, the country had embarked on a public policy of systematically deinstitutionalizing the mentally ill, believing they could do much better if they received treatment, including necessary medication, through nonresidential community mental health centers. But the vision was only partially realized. Many mentally ill people were not getting the help or medications they needed. We now had thousands of mentally ill living on our streets, under bridges, and, with some frequency, committing crimes. As a result, prisons had become our new mental health institutions.

As a prison administrator, it was a constant battle to get legislators and public policy makers to recognize this reality and appropriate funds for necessary treatment and psychotropic medications. Even when the response was that the mentally ill criminals were "where they belong," we argued we needed the treatment funding to better provide for the safety of our prison employees. The courts were of considerable help in ordering mental health treatment as a result of conditions of confinement lawsuits brought after lawmakers refused to act. But the public policy battle continues.

I join the general public in their skepticism about mental health defenses to culpability for criminal behavior. My career in prosecution has convinced me that, while a large number of criminals are mentally ill, very few are insane and unaware of the wrongfulness of their conduct. The vast majority of mentally ill people I encountered were susceptible to principles of deterrence. If I had the ability to design a system from scratch, I would make some significant modifications. I would abolish the not guilty by reason of insanity defense. The prosecutor would make a threshold decision whether to charge a mentally ill person with a crime. If charged, I would simply allow any defendant to pose their mental illness as a defense. They could claim that because of their mental illness they were incapable of forming the state of mind necessary to commit the crime. If they were acquitted of a serious crime on the basis of such an assertion of mental illness, or if the prosecutor declined to prosecute because of it, the district attorney or some other designated official could commence a civil action to have the defendant committed to a mental hospital or ordered to undergo appropriate treatment. All persons convicted of crimes, despite the assertion of mental illness, would receive the prescribed statutory sentence, including prison when appropriate. But if the sentencing judge or prison administrator deemed it advisable, the defendant would be housed in a facility within the Department of Corrections specifically designed to deal with the mentally ill. The cost of such a system would be considerably higher than at present. While prison systems currently have mental health units, they typically serve only a small portion of inmates needing such services. We would essentially be recreating some of the mental health institutions that we systematically dismantled in earlier decades, but we would still be investing heavily in community mental health centers to prevent the mentally ill from committing crimes in the first place. In fact, I believe the high cost of adequately treating mentally ill criminals might force policy makers to adequately fund community health centers.

My vision is theoretical and unlikely to gain popularity anytime soon. There would be serious opposition from many in the mental health community and prison reform advocates who believe prisons are no place for the mentally ill, regardless of what crimes they've committed and regardless of what treatment is available. The public may well rebel at learning the cost of actually treating mentally ill criminals. But, as a bottom line, I believe we need a system in which the mentally ill are held properly accountable for their crimes and the public is adequately protected from them, but which doesn't ignore the fact that they are mentally ill and in need of treatment. I'm quite certain it could be handled better than it is at present.

IX. No Higher Calling

The justice system cannot work without prosecutors who competently review evidence, make principled charging decisions, and who zealously but fairly pursue conviction and just punishment.

All the lawyers involved in the criminal justice system believe they have a high calling. Defense attorneys protect the rights of the accused, who are cloaked with the presumption of innocence, and make the government prove its case before their client loses their freedom or has their forehead stamped with a *C* (for criminal) for the rest of his life. They naturally see themselves as defending the citizen accused from the awesome power of the government. Judges are the referees who assure that both sides adhere to the prescribed rules and that the contest proceeds fairly by adjudicating the constant skirmishes that occur between the parties. At its conclusion and upon conviction, the judge is looked to for Solomon-like wisdom in imposing a fair punishment within the bounds of discretion afforded by the legislature. So, judges, like defense attorneys, can rightly view themselves as indispensable to justice.

But there can be no justice unless someone takes wrongdoers to task in the first place. Edmund Burke said, "All that is necessary for evil to triumph is for good men and women to do nothing." I have been known to tell my fellow prosecutors a revised version. "All that is necessary for evil to triumph is lazy and incompetent prosecutors." An instructor at the first prosecutor training class I attended in 1977 put it this way: "Prosecution is no place for dilettantes and part-timers." The justice system cannot work without prosecutors who competently review evidence, make principled charging decisions, and who zealously but fairly pursue conviction and just punishment.

Even die-hard defense advocates concede the point. In his book *Letters to a Young Lawyer*, Alan Dershowitz, a frequent critic of prosecutors, acknowledged that

> there are few higher callings than an honest prosecutor with a real sense of justice. Such a prosecutor can have a greater impact on the criminal justice system than any defense lawyer or judge…A good prosecutor can help an innocent defendant more effectively than most defense attorneys can, by insisting that the evidence be solid and that police and prosecutors comply with their ethical obligations. A decent prosecutor can also help a guilty defendant, by exercising discretion to charge him with an appropriate crime and to seek a reasonable sentence.[*]

As indicated earlier in the book, the ability of prosecutors to represent the public interest, as opposed to the special interest of an individual or organizational client, is unique in the law. To stand before a court and proudly proclaim that you appear "on behalf of the people of the State of Colorado" or "for the United States of America" is a daunting privilege and responsibility. Yet, at the same time, prosecutors can experience the immense satisfaction that comes with vindicating the interests of the individual victim of a terrible crime. I know both police detectives and prosecutors who carry in their wallets the photos of murder victims in cases they're trying to solve or successfully prosecute. They're well aware that if

[*] Alan Dershowitz, *Letters to a Young Lawyer* (Basic Books, 2001), 150.

they don't hold the evildoer accountable, there will be no earthly accountability for the crime.

I've noticed another phenomenon that says a great deal about the experience of being a prosecutor. I've talked to a lot of very successful lawyers who were prosecutors earlier in their career—lawyers who now make lots of money in private practice and lawyers who are now highly esteemed judges on the state or federal bench. Almost to a person, they freely acknowledge that the time they spent as a prosecutor was the most fun they've had as a lawyer and oftentimes the most meaningful experience they've had as a lawyer. They typically indicate that they've never recaptured the collegiality and sense of teamwork they felt as a prosecutor. When I was a young lawyer, I was skeptical about such assertions. But not anymore. As U.S. attorney, I regularly interviewed successful lawyers who were willing to give up incomes of $200,000 to $500,000 to come to work as an assistant U.S. attorney for $100,000 per year. They had come to the conclusion they needed to make the change to put greater meaning into their life as a lawyer. As attorney general, I've hired several successful veteran lawyers who are seeking to recapture the collegiality and sense of purpose that only a public law office can give them.

This raises the question of whether lawyers are more effective as prosecutors when they do it as a career or during a limited tenure. I have these observations: A good public prosecution office needs both career prosecutors and committed and enthusiastic lawyers who want to serve as a prosecutor temporarily on their way to other legal pursuits. Career prosecutors bring the wisdom of experience, the institutional memory, and the sense of proportion and fairness that every good public law office must have and can only get from a veteran of many battles. But a constant supply of bright and eager noncareerists is essential to give a public law office creativity and vitality. You need lawyers to ask good questions and lawyers to give good answers. An office with too few career prosecutors can be overzealous and inconsistent. An office that's too heavy with career prosecutors can become staid, bureaucratic, and lacking in passion.

The sacrifices involved in a career in prosecution aren't just financial. I've lost some friends as a result of carrying out my obligations as a prosecutor. Even the social lives of my wife and children have been affected somewhat. On a number of occasions, I've had genuine concerns about threats made to my personal safety. Phone calls in the middle of the night can become routine. But I, like most prosecutors, long ago concluded that the rewards of working as a prosecutor far exceeded the liabilities.

Personally, I'm glad I spent thirteen years of my career outside of prosecution. Not only were those financially rewarding years, but my ten years in private practice, in particular, gave me greater perspective about what opportunities the law affords and the unique opportunities for job satisfaction found in prosecution. Many career prosecutors don't fully recognize how lucky they are to have broad and noble responsibilities beyond the interests of an individual client. I believe I have a much greater appreciation for the prosecution function than I would have had I not spent many years doing something else.

More so than in private practice, I found that being a district attorney, U.S. attorney, and attorney general gave me a pulpit outside of the courtroom as well. In those capacities, I have given more than fifteen hundred speeches to groups ranging from two people to ten thousand people. I've talked about subjects ranging from leadership and character to criminal justice reform to the intricacies of admitting certain forensic evidence. The views I've expressed in all those public appearances give a pretty accurate picture of who I am and what my values are. I've appeared before legislative committees more than seventy times and influenced legislation on juvenile crime, the insanity defense, the death penalty, Internet safety, and many other matters. The ability to impact events outside the courtroom, as well as inside, makes the prosecutor's job even more challenging and rewarding.

As in most occupations, when you reflect back on a prosecution career, you tend to remember personalities more than events. It's people who really make life meaningful and interesting, at home and on the job. And so it is with my prosecution career. I've been privileged to work with people of great character and unwavering purpose, with people of high integrity who brought passion to the task of pursuing justice. They were my superiors, my peers, and my subordinates. People sometimes chuckle when I tell them that the most virtuous people I've met tend to be lawyers, politicians, or both. But I'm completely serious. And so many of them were prosecutors.

I've done many things in my life—most of which I'm very content with. I'm happy to be the husband of my wonderful wife, Janet, for thirty-two years now. I'm proud to be the father of Alison and Kate, two incredibly intelligent and talented young women. And I'm very proud to be a lawyer. Despite the public's image of the profession, I've found it one with incredible opportunities to help people and to advance the human condition. I'm proud of all the various tasks I have pursued as a lawyer, including the private representation of many worthy clients. I have absolutely no regrets that I chose to pursue a legal career, but I'm not sure I could say that so unequivocally if I hadn't spent eighteen years as a prosecutor. I'm truly privileged to have had the high honor and responsibility of serving as the chief prosecutor on the local, state, and federal level. In the vast universe of occupational undertakings, I don't believe there's any higher calling, any greater trust, or any greater responsibility than to serve the citizens of your community as a public prosecutor.

About the Author

John W. Suthers has spent his thirty-year legal career in the U.S. justice system, including service as an elected district attorney, a presidentially appointed U.S. attorney, and as Colorado's attorney general since 2005. He also ran Colorado's correctional system from 1999 until 2001. Handling a wide variety of cases—ranging from drunk driving to murder and from petty theft to billion-dollar securities fraud—has given him a unique perspective on how the justice system works and how it might be improved. A graduate of Notre Dame and the University of Colorado Law School, Suthers is an adjunct professor of law at the University of Denver. A lifetime resident of Colorado, he currently lives in Colorado Springs with his wife, Janet.

More thought-provoking titles
in the Speaker's Corner series

Beyond Cowboy Politics
Colorado and the New West
  Adam Schrager, Sam Scinta, and Shannon Hassan, editors

Brave New World of Health Care
What Every American Needs to Know about the Impending Health Care Crisis
  Richard D. Lamm

Condition Critical
A New Moral Vision for Health Care
  Richard D. Lamm and Robert H. Blank

Daddy On Board
Parenting Roles for the 21st Century
  Dottie Lamm

Ethics for a Finite World
An Essay Concerning a Sustainable Future
  Herschel Elliott

God and Caesar in America
An Essay on Religion and Politics
  Gary Hart

One Nation Under Guns
An Essay on an American Epidemic
  Arnold Grossman

On the Clean Road Again
Biodiesel and the Future of the Family Farm
  Willie Nelson

Parting Shots from My Brittle Bow
Reflections on American Politics and Life
  Eugene J. McCarthy

Power of the People
America's New Electricity Choices
  Carol Sue Tombari

Social Security and the Golden Age
An Essay on the New American Demographic
   George McGovern

A Solitary War
A Diplomat's Chronicle of the Iraq War and Its Lessons
   Heraldo Muñoz

Stop Global Warming
The Solution Is You!
   Laurie David

TABOR and Direct Democracy
An Essay on the End of the Republic
   Bradley J. Young

Think for Yourself!
An Essay on Cutting through the Babble, the Bias, and the Hype
   Steve Hindes

Two Wands, One Nation
An Essay on Race and Community in America
   Richard D. Lamm

Under the Eagle's Wing
A National Security Strategy of the United States for 2009
   Gary Hart

A Vision for 2012
Planning for Extraordinary Change
   John L. Petersen

For more information, visit www.fulcrumbooks.com